Kent Vol II
Edited by Kelly Oliver

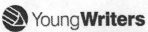

First published in Great Britain in 2004 by:
Young Writers
Remus House
Coltsfoot Drive
Peterborough
PE2 9JX
Telephone: 01733 890066
Website: www.youngwriters.co.uk

All Rights Reserved

© Copyright Contributors 2004

SB ISBN 1 84460 401 2

Foreword

This year, the Young Writers' 'Poetry In Motion' competition proudly presents a showcase of the best poetic talent selected from over 40,000 up-and-coming writers nationwide.

Young Writers was established in 1991 to promote the reading and writing of poetry within schools and to the youth of today. Our books nurture and inspire confidence in the ability of young writers and provide a snapshot of poems written in schools and at home by budding poets of the future.

The thought effort, imagination and hard work put into each poem impressed us all and the task of selecting poems was a difficult but nevertheless enjoyable experience.

We hope you are as pleased as we are with the final selection and that you and your family continue to be entertained with *Poetry In Motion Kent Vol II* for many years to come.

Contents

    Tasneef Mahammad (12)   1
    Ryan Perrins (12)   2

Bexley Grammar School
    Nathan Lampen (13)   2
    Joshua Crittenden (14)   3
    David Stevens (13)   3
    Sam Fisher (13)   4
    Lucy MacDonald (14)   4
    Adeyinka Roy-Macauley (13)   5
    Kelsey Williams (13)   6
    Tom Lynch (13)   6
    Scott Moore (13)   7
    Sophie Haslam   8
    Alex Tolfree (13)   9
    Tom Tarling (13)   9
    Sunny Briah (13)   10
    Konjiwe Mutambirwa (13)   11
    Daniel Sydee (13)   11

Borden Grammar School
    Adam Clark (16)   12
    Samuel Mumford (13)   12
    Jonathan Sharman (16)   13
    Natalie Donovan (17)   14
    Dean Brown (13)   14
    Harrison Fry (16)   15
    David Walker (14)   15
    James Forster (16)   16
    James Herbert (14)   17
    Patrick Smith (13)   17
    Chris McGee (16)   18
    Ben Comery (14)   18
    James Cross (13)   19
    Michael Baxendale (15)   20
    Simon Cuthbert (13)   20
    Callum Essam (13)   21
    Johnathan Rudland (13)   21

Jordan Ingram (13)	22
Samuel Williamson (13)	22
Richard Moakes (13)	23
Andrew Walker (13)	24
James Bowen (13)	24
Robert Burton (13)	25
Patrick Hall (13)	25
Tom Woolnough (14)	26
Matthew Jordan (14)	26
George Packer (14)	27
Sam Duchesne (12)	27
Daniel Campbell (14)	28
Michael Phillips (14)	28
Stuart Brown (14)	29
Laurence Billing (14)	29
Gareth Messenger (12)	30
Jack Mundy (14)	30
Ben Lane (12)	31
Sam Thomas (12)	31
Ryan Rook (14)	32
Nathan Foster (12)	32
Declan Cornelius (12)	33
Liam Ward (12)	33
Lee Rogers (12)	34
Christopher Jenkins (13)	34
Dominic Campbell (12)	35
Ahmet Eken (12)	35
Liam O'Donoghue (12)	36
Matthew Ingram (12)	36
Patrick Collins (12)	37
Luke Bowerman (12)	37
Ben Nappey (13)	38
Michael Friar (12)	39
Luke Grubb (12)	40
Will Halls (12)	41

Bradbourne School

Vindhya Parasher (13)	41
Rebecca Nicholls (13)	42
Nicola Smith (13)	42
Eloise Macdonald-Meyer (11)	43

Faye Purchase (11)	43
Chloë Robinson (13)	44
Danielle Pyrah (11)	44
Lizzie Hasler (13)	45
Justine Fedorowycz (13)	45
Hayley Dean (11)	46
Lily Fleet-Newman (11)	46
Lauren Medhurst (11)	46
Siân Cunningham (13)	47
Laura Sparks (13)	48
Caris Strain (11)	48
Bethany Lynch (11)	49
Charlotte Farrugia (13)	49
Sophie Fordham (11)	50
Vanessa Gbadebo (11)	50
Kelly Bryant (13)	51
Ellen Tout (13)	51
Kayleigh Jarrett (13)	52
Bianca Lefevre (11)	52
Tina Smith-Reeve (13)	53
Becky Bailey (13)	54
Jessika Cruse (11)	55
Natasha Bray (11)	55

Dorton House School For The Blind

Nic Taylor (12)	55
Kirsten Read (15)	56
Abdul Hameed (15)	56
Hammad Husain (15)	57
Emma Galvin (15)	57
Charlotte Davey-Whiting (13)	58
Daniel McGee (14)	59
Josie Hammond (12)	59
James Neate (15)	60
Matthew Cleave (14)	60
Lottie Smith (15)	61
Bradley Pilkington (14)	61
Jack Blackmore (12)	62
Christine Payne (14)	63
Hayleigh Rayment (14)	64

Furness Special School
Sam Coomber (12)	64
James Ruane (12)	65
Louis Vincent (12)	65
Daniel Taylor (11)	65

Homewood School
Jennifer Brockwell (12)	66
Sam Boxall (12)	66
Robert Button (12)	67
Mikala Brown (13)	67
Thomas Bushell (12)	68
Becky Budgen (12)	68
Catherine Clothier (12)	69
James Cornish (12)	69
Jessica Cooper (12)	70
Stephanie Chibnall (12)	70
Frankie Crane (12)	71
Anna Bagulay (12)	71
Becky Bell (12)	72
Fergus Campbell (12)	72
Hannah Davis (12)	73
Robert Crawford (12)	73
Gavin Curtin (12)	74
Samantha Batt (12)	74
Billy Beaney (12)	75
Jenna Bertram (12)	75
Jessica Grimes (13)	76
Jodie Blake (12)	76
Charlotte Griffiths (12)	77
Terry Bourne (12)	77
Leanne Dolman (12)	78
Chris Bottrill (12)	78
Stephanie Adams (12)	79
Alice Doucy (12)	79
Robert Antrum (12)	80
Blue Jenkins (11)	80
Vickie Fuller (12)	81
Adam Giles (12)	81
Samantha Gibbons (12)	82
William Alkin (12)	82

Rebecca Greenfield (12)	83
Jade Farrin (12)	83
Matthew Hogg (12)	84
Elouise Ellis (12)	84
Joshua Earland (12)	85
Aiden Gorham (12)	85
Russell Dullaway (12)	85
Danielle Groat (12)	86
Jaime Golding (12)	86
Amy Guess (13)	87
Joshua Dunk (12)	87
Ben Hawkes (12)	88
Nabil Graham (12)	88
Amy Hilding (12)	89
Sophie Hilden (12)	89
Rhys Maynard (12)	90
Sophie Goldstein (12)	90
Martyn Luck (12)	91
David Lincoln (13)	91
Lizzie Phipps (12)	92
Harry Higginson (12)	92
Daniel Oliver (12)	93
Eleanor Hayward (12)	93
Matthew Mansfield (12)	94
Billy Hands (12)	94
Michael Rice (12)	94
Megan Lee (12)	95
Michael Laity (13)	95
Michelle King (11)	96
Gabrielle McNamara (12)	97
Tom Wood (12)	97
Jade Pearman (12)	98
Kirsty Parsons (12)	98
Rachel White (14)	99
Amy Neil (12)	99
Charlotte Wyatt (13)	100
David Neill (12)	100
Fleur Schrapel (12)	101
Alice Murton (12)	101
Adrian Worsley (12)	102
Dylan Troeger (12)	102
Oliver Sargeant (12)	103

Ben Squires Quinn (13)   103
Freya Walker (12)   104
Kiefer Sim (12)   105
Ben Vincer (13)   106
Jonathan White (12)   106
Hollie Weatherill (12)   107
Daniel Warren (12)   108

Mascalls School

Tom Eaton (11)   108
Victoria Mayrick (11)   109
Christina Bridger (12)   109
Billie Pingault (11)   110
Katie Davison (12)   110
Rebekka Chamberlain (12)   111
Jasmin Allen (11)   111
Amy Prior (11)   112
Natasha Nichols (11)   112
Nick McKee (12)   113
Adam El-Bir (12)   113
Hayley Sterling (11)   114
George Willock (11)   114
Alex Flegg (12)   115
Laura Gledhill (12)   115
Emily Milton (11)   116
Katherine Whalesby (12)   116
Georgia Hebborn (12)   117
Carolyn Bassett (11)   117
Beverley Williams (12)   118
Hasna Miah (12)   118
Carys Nicholls (12)   119
Megan Lumley (12)   119
Susie Collings (13)   120
Nathalie Hill (13)   121
Kirsty Hill (12)   122
Abbie Collins (11)   122
Emma Shrimpton (13)   123

Meadows School

Josephine Shaw (12)   123
Ashley Lockyer (15)   124

Tanya McCarthy (14)	124
David Killick (13)	125
Aaron Peters (15)	125
Allan Cole (14)	126
Ann-Marie Telfer (14)	126
Nathan Lahrar (13)	127
Luke Dorey (14)	128
Kieran Grant (14)	128
Lee Mackay (15)	128
Karl White (15)	129

Minster College

Nathalie Gunn (15)	129
Emma Mason (13) & Lucy Parish (14)	130
Laura Gregory (13)	130
Claire Whitaker (14)	131
Jamie McCombie (15)	131
Brian Thain (13)	132
Daniel Goodwin (14)	132
Kirsty Elmes (15)	133
Luke Brown (13)	133
Stacey Norris (14)	134
Charlotte Gath (13)	134
Nicholas Miles (14)	135
Jeydon Fletcher (14)	135
Carly-Louise Fagg (14)	136
Tara Chapman (13)	137
Chloe Bates (14)	138
Kasi Richardson (13)	138
Wesley Connor (14)	139
Adam Wilson (15)	139
Carla Feist (13)	140
Charlotte Rowe (14)	140
Matthew Gearing (13)	141
Ross Allwright (16)	141
Stephanie Collins (13)	142
Sarah Dear (13)	143
Amy Hall (14)	143
Robert Piper (13)	144
Thomas Hewitt (13)	144
Aaron Clark (13)	145

Hannah Payne (15)	146
Cherie Simpson (13)	146
Paul Young (13)	147
Natalie Crossley (13)	147
Lizzie Martin (15)	148
Michael Batchelor (13)	148
Fiona West (13)	149
Rebecca Penman (16)	149
Aaron Gray (15)	150
Craig Allen (13)	150
Omer Mertdogdu (15)	151
Carl Carolan (13)	151

St Mary & St Joseph's School, Sidcup

Vinson Lee (15)	152
Irene Muiruri (11)	153
Georgina Lampen (13)	154
Nadine Ijewere (11)	154
Anthony Manzi (13)	155
Nichola Mitchell (13)	155
Eugen Sagalla (11)	156
Joshua Bonhill Smith (11)	156
Danielle Sullivan (11)	157
Deborah Obaseki (11)	157
Christopher Collinge (12)	158
Charlie Ward (11)	158
Katie Gianakakis (11)	159
Matthew Foy (13)	159
Stacey Rump (11)	160
Sian Ciara Seymour (11)	161
Georgina Heneghan (11)	162
Sam Leonard (13)	163
Ben Faurie (12)	163
Michelle Besa (11)	164
Heidi Pullig (13)	164
Shaun Egan (11)	165
Rachel Johnston (11)	165
Adam Hardie (11)	166
Alfie Clark (11)	166
Cherrelle Morgan (13)	167
Rebecca McCormack (12)	168

Jimmy Hicks (14)	168
Patricia Abidakun (11)	169
Rhianne Supple (12)	169
Ronnie Gleeson (11)	170
Christopher Lynch (11)	170
Conor Cooper (12)	171
Rosie Major (11)	171
Ciaran O'Mahony (11)	172
Christopher Loughlin (11)	172
Joshua Nwanazia (13)	173
Stephanie Jaques (14)	174
Sarah Jeffrey (12)	174
Georgia Lynne Mae Bocanog (16)	175
Henry Sivell (14)	176
Joseph Duggan (13)	176
Rachelle Bocanog (14)	177
Tim Masera (12)	177
Shauna McDonagh (13)	178
Sam Edwards (11)	178
Chris Pullig (13)	179
Sinead Connolly (12)	179
Bose Bakare (13)	180
Laura Sugrue (13)	181
Jade Murphy (14)	182
Philip Streete (13)	183
Isabel Irarrázaval (13)	184
Kelly Marrington (12)	185
Jenny Faurie (13)	186
Noëleen Spiteri (13)	186
Tom Kelleher (12)	187
Kieran McCarthy (13)	187
Sesugh Angula (11)	188
Ben Hudson (13)	188
Leanne Powley (13)	189
Angela Gladding (13)	189
Joseph Chapman (12)	190

The Grammar School For Girls, Wilmington

Naomi Russell (13)	190

Tunbridge Wells Grammar School For Boys

Sean Wright (11)	191
William Ottway (12)	191
Howard Rickard (12)	192
Michael Wilkinson (11)	192
Nathan Durrant (11)	193
Matthew Watts (12)	193
Paul Weatherall (11)	194
Dean Weller (11)	195
Peter Tubb (11)	195
Matthew Woodgate (11)	196
Daniel Wood (12)	196
Jamie Watson (12)	197
Alan Wanders (11)	197
Sam Dowson (11)	198
Jamie Gill (12)	198
Christopher Davies (11)	199
Benjamin Watts (12)	200
Andrew Skiller (12)	201
Will Tompsett (12)	201
Nicholas Wallis (11)	202
James Yardley (11)	202
George Fisk (11)	203
James Dorricott (11)	203
Sam Tanner (12)	204
Alex Dove (12)	205
Jonathan Woolley (11)	206
Robert Whittaker (11)	206
Michael Smith (13)	207
Philip Tremenheere (12)	207
Michael Lever (12)	208
George Williams (11)	208
Kristian Wilson (11)	209
George Cramer-Todd (11)	209
Shaun Drury (11)	210
Tim Riley (13)	211
Dominic Tunstill (11)	212
Ed Brooks (12)	213
William Bailey & Declan D'Arcy (12)	214
Andrew Wood (11)	214
Edward Hallford-Nye (13)	215

Jake Bambrough (12)	215
Max Richards	216
Calum Duncan (11)	217
Cameron Dall (12)	218
Oliver Ward (11)	218
Matthew Grainger (12)	219
Tom Watson (11)	220
Michael Ells (13)	220
Jack Stookes (12)	221
Tom Parrish (12)	222
Ted Sardar (13)	222
Roger King (12)	223
Joshua Brice (12)	223
Phil Selwood (13)	224
Michael Hodges (12)	225
Andrew Brown (13)	226
Thomas Wood (12)	226
Daniel Francis (12)	227
Tim Drake Brockman (11)	227
James Perrett (13)	228
Daniel Edgson Wright (12)	228
Sam Gregson-Williams (12)	229
Mark Eastwood (11)	229
Alex d'Albertanson (12)	230
Will Moore (12)	231
Stephen Dale (11)	231
Gordon Rieck (14)	232
Alex Day (11)	233
Ryan Welby (11)	234
John Bone (12)	234
Declan Ellis (11)	235
Thomas Williams (11)	235
Jamie Craig (11)	236
Henry Everett (11)	237
Richard Fallon (12)	238
Michael Dobereiner (11)	239
Ben Dahmen (11)	240
Alan Haugh (12)	241
Aaron Fariba (12)	242
Christopher Farrell (11)	243
Frank Anthony Ward (11)	244
Henry Dolling (11)	245

Walthamstow Hall
   Hazel Levett (14)   245
   Lauren Watson (14)   246
   Gemma Cottis (12)   247
   Stephanie Pickerill (14)   248
   Tanwen Evans (11)   248
   Jessica Wrigley (11)   249
   Rosalind Mayes (13)   249
   Gillian McCusker (15)   250
   Rosie Buist (12)   251
   Abbie Kemsley (14)   252
   Lucy Low (13)   253
   Miranda Kitchener (12)   253
   Rachel Bullen (12)   254
   Gabi Groves (13)   254
   Francesca Warrington (14)   255

The Poems

Hard Life

I saw a lot of homicide,
I've walked ghettos where thugs collide,
Young kinds run for their lives or hide
People trying to survive gun wars, many have died,
So we have to have dignity and pride,
Too many mothers crying until their eyes were dried.
So the relation to the poem is that we've got to make a rotation,
All I need for this message is a little concentration,
So many youngsters die, maybe babies even pretty soon thugs
    will wipe out the whole nation
And the thirst of the poor is maybe caused by evaporation,
But if they go the wrong way about it, they'll end up in the police station
It's getting annoying like a bad rash,
Why do people talk trash to get cash?
People victimise from toes to the eyelash, it's too dark so
    we need the light to flash.
So why do people do these things, it's all psychology
And why people explain physically and get involved with biology,
But some talents are used for good things like immunology.
Since my birth on this Earth I knew the sustainer of the sun and
    the moon,
Pretty soon most of the hard-working students would be immune.
People are freezing cold,
Most of them never die old,
So who is bold enough to overpower me and this truth I hold?

Tasneef Mahammad (12)

Acrostic

I can eat a whole pizza on my own. Mum gets the extra
L arge thick one.
I t still doesn't fill me up. I like the soft base, not too hard.
K ing size pepperoni with lots of
E xtra

P ineapple, ham and cheese.
I eat in my bed - so full, drop off to sleep.
Z *zzzzzz*
Z *zzzzzz*
A nd good night!

Ryan Perrins (12)

Ghost Poem

Say it's the leaves, the way they rustle.
Say it's a shadow or the scraping of a stick.
Childhood friends, dead and buried.

They're out there now, small ghosts,
Who never knew when enough was enough,
One who ran into a car, one who tripped?

One on a stone and fell on a stick that poked
Through his heart. Lost and forgotten,
They've gone into the unknown!

Nathan Lampen (13)
Bexley Grammar School

Clad In Velvet

Audaciously clad in velvet he went into the night,
The all-consuming blackness depleted sound and sight.
The velvet smothered character walked on none-the-less,
The ghostly, ghoulish figurines concealed within his vest.
At his destination he withdrew a silver crest,
Upon this gleaming emblem the figurines did rest.
Shouting foreign tongue he called upon the God,
'Bring alive my sinful kin and watch us steal their blood!'
And so they did with light and fire and all their bitterness,
But now this story comes to death their locations one could not guess.

Joshua Crittenden (14)
Bexley Grammar School

The Attic

Sam was about to open his bedroom door,
But then he heard something shuffling on the floor,
Up in the attic he heard a strange creak,
Then he heard a very loud shriek,
He went upstairs to explore,
Then someone opened the attic door,
Something was staring at him face to face,
And then it started walking at a slow pace,
Around the figure was a laser beam,
Then he woke up and realised it was a dream.

David Stevens (13)
Bexley Grammar School

On The Stroke Of Midnight

The rusty gate creaked in agony as I entered the graveyard,
A black mist covered the full moon
It was dark, black as pitch,
The thunder boomed, the wind roared.
The werewolves howled, the bats shrieked.
Leaves crushed under my feet as I tiptoed towards the 'the coffin'.
My blood ran cold and I was filled with fear.
The coffin opened with a bang,
I was startled and dropped my torch.
I waited . . .
. . . nothing.
I saw a shadow out of the corner of my eye.
I turned, 'Who's there?'
A ray of light shone on the coffin,
A new day had begun.

Sam Fisher (13)
Bexley Grammar School

The Graveyard

The graveyard is abandoned
Lowly and rotting; it's left to decay.
But it's only left by humans
Not by the undead . . .

A howl echoes through the gravestones
Ever chanting its gruesome call
The owner of the call is unknown
Zombie or werewolf? Take your pick
For this graveyard is home for both.

Once this graveyard used to be normal.
Surrounded in bluebells and shiny railings.
What kind of transformation has taken place
To show the complete opposite?

Lucy MacDonald (14)
Bexley Grammar School

Long Gone

The gun was fired, *bang!*
The bullet shot out like nothing else can,
The man was gone,
Long gone.

Happy, sad, relieved emotions through your body,
All of a sudden a cold feeling washes those emotions away,
Your heart beats faster,
'Is this right?'

Things go through your mind,
'What's happening to me?'
You wonder as all of a sudden you go stiff with fear,
'This can't be right . . . can it?'

You see a shadow move,
But there is nobody around,
Only you and the dead body are left,
Then it hits you.

'It's his ghost,' you say as you regain control of your body,
You search aimlessly,
No one, only silence,
Eerie silence.

'Leave me be,' you say,
'You're dead, you can't be here,
You don't scare me,
You annoy me.'

'You won't annoy me any more,'
You pick up the gun,
Place it to your head,
'You won't annoy me any more.'

The gun is fired, *bang!*
The bullet shot out like nothing else can,
You are gone,
Long gone.

Adeyinka Roy-Macauley (13)
Bexley Grammar School

Here Today, Gone Tomorrow

The dark trees, towering over me,
as I walk through the maze of undergrowth.
Through the mist I see a silhouette
and the hairs on the back of my neck rise.

Looking around through the darkness of this place,
I turn quickly and quicken my pace.
Is death through the mist?
Am I next on his list?

The sound of hooves alerts my senses,
all five of which go into overdrive.
I become aware of owls screeching,
the smell of mud, mixed strangely with blood.

I hear bells ringing in my ears,
dying here now, is my greatest fear.
Is this the last time I will see the moon?
Death cannot come now, it is far too soon.

But I have no choice, death is here,
something warm on my face, is it a tear?
Silver shines in the darkness, it seems far away,
will I be here tomorrow, will I even last today?

Kelsey Williams (13)
Bexley Grammar School

The Haunted House

There I was in the house,
But this house is a little odd.
It is a haunted house,
When I entered it was all fine,
But when at night,
You're sure of a fright,
As the ghosts and ghouls come out,
But when you hear a bump in the night,
Could it be the ghosts ready to scare?

Tom Lynch (13)
Bexley Grammar School

The Shadow

On the night of the full moon,
Everyone stays at home,
No one dares venture out,
Or else they'll be doomed.

The Shadow is a fearsome beast,
It will suck out your soul,
It lurks at the crossroads,
Waiting for a victim.

A freezing cold swirls around it,
Rooting you to the spot,
It envelops you in a deathly shroud,
Where your screams cannot be heard.

Scariest of all is its malevolent glare,
Fiery and blazing,
Just one look and you will find,
You have just lost your mind.

It can be conquered however,
But there is only one way,
It is challenging and difficult
And a group of you must do it.

You must link hands and form a circle around it,
Then sing happy songs and hymns,
This will drive the beast mad
And will rid you of it forever.

On the night of the full moon,
Everyone stays at home,
No one dares venture out,
Or else they'll be doomed.

Scott Moore (13)
Bexley Grammar School

The Streets Of Dartford Moor

The *murky* streets of Dartford Moor,
Not a soul has touched them in years!
The legends of murders and ghostly spirits,
Has left many people in tears!
With its pebbled streets - covered in ice
And ancient houses - infested with mice!
These are the streets of Dartford Moor!

The silent streets of Dartford Moor,
Takes place in the breath of the night!
The only sound to be heard is the wind
And the silence is brought on by fright!
With its eerie atmosphere - controlled by the spirits
And God's preachers - repeating his lyrics!
These are the streets of Dartford Moor!

The dull streets of Dartford Moor,
Not a primary colour in sight!
Covered in blacks and browns and greys,
Refusing to invite any light!
With its silver door handles - covered in dust
And running water - smelling of must!
These are the streets of Dartford Moor!

I've told you once, but never again,
About the streets of Dartford Moor!
If you still wish to explore its dreaded alleys
Go ahead, just remember - *you've been warned!*

Sophie Haslam
Bexley Grammar School

Anyone?

The wind whistled through the dark room,
The fire crackled fiercely in the fireplace,
The floorboard creaked louder, louder,
Is anyone there?

An eerie owl's hoot echoed round the room,
The chandelier swung on the ceiling, dusty cobwebs falling from it,
My heart beat faster, faster,
Is anyone there?

The crimson curtains blew wildly in the ancient, wooden window frame,
Shadows danced creepily on the ceiling,
Making peculiar patterns and shapes,
The flames flickered brighter, brighter,
Is anyone there?

Alex Tolfree (13)
Bexley Grammar School

The Obelisk Poem

Outside the old, wrecked house
Stands a red obelisk
I often stand and wonder about supernatural things
The windows and door uncannily resemble a face

An eerie light shines from the windows at night
And things seem to move, maybe spectral beings.
At the dead of night I can hear music, a phantom piano player?
The unearthly house seems to be totally inhabited by ghosts!

As I walk past the house I shiver
It's as if the obelisk radiates cold
I walk up to the obelisk and touch it . . .
I am thrown backwards by an unseen force.

Tom Tarling (13)
Bexley Grammar School

He Is All Alone

Can you see that man?
That elderly, solitary, secluded man - drifting along at a snail's pace?
Yes?
He is all alone.

He has no friends, no family.
They're all dead - just memories - he is the only person that he knows.
He is all alone.

In his heart, he wishes was dead.
In his heart, he is dead.
His friends are all around him,
He can't speak to them or hear them.
He is all alone.

Sometimes he feels them,
He knows they're there;
They're just waiting,
They want to communicate, to say 'hello'.
He is all alone.

Can you see that man?
That elderly, solitary, secluded man - drifting along at a snail's pace?
No?
Is he alone?

He took his life the other day,
He couldn't bear the wait,
Now his friends speak, they say, 'Hello.'
He is not alone.

Sunny Briah (13)
Bexley Grammar School

Are You Safe?

You are walking alone,
It is dark and there is no one around.
You can feel the soft, warm earth,
Shudder beneath the tarmac.

It is a warm, cosy night,
But something icy slithers,
Down your spine.
Leaving you in a state of trauma.

The hairs on your neck stand up,
Goosebumps emerge slowly from your skin.
You start walking faster!
But why?

Is there someone behind you?
Why can you feel the presence of someone near you?
Are you safe?
Who is there?
Don't turn around.

Konjiwe Mutambirwa (13)
Bexley Grammar School

The Cat

Creeping in the shadows
Always unseen and unheard
Finding somewhere to go
Hunting for some mice or a bird.

A cold-blooded killer
Hunting with sharp teeth and claws
Nothing stalks quieter;
Defying the gravity laws.

After all the murder
It stealthily heads back home;
Curls up on its master -
Nightly activities unknown.

Daniel Sydee (13)
Bexley Grammar School

Together As Always

Together as always,
United they stand,
Picking on the weak and helpless,
But not hand in hand.

Together as always,
With no leader of the group,
Everyone as equals,
This is their truth.

Together as always,
For each other no task too tall,
In their eyes the key is survival,
At a game where the weak will fall.

Together as always,
Yet spiteful to the bone,
As this pack of wolves,
Never run alone!

Adam Clark (16)
Borden Grammar School

All Out For 50!

The bowler ran up clenching the seam,
The batsmen stood up to face the ball,
It pitched low and was travelling fast,
The batsmen stepped out of his crease a good four yards,
He played his shot but mistimed it and watched the ball fly past,
The wicket keeper waited eagerly and caught the ball,
Then whipped off the bails and yelled, *'Howzzat!'*
Up went the finger of the umpire and that was that.

Samuel Mumford (13)
Borden Grammar School

The Wrath Of Winter's Night

Frost lined
The world lies still
While ice grows
Upon its sleeping face.

And glistens
In the icy light
From the stars that lie
Like frost upon the darkened sky.

And far below
Beneath their icy gaze
The rivers choke
And streams stand still.

Nowhere to run
Beneath the branches bare
Not dressed in emerald leaf
But a gown of deathly white.

As beautiful and bleak
As winter's chilling stare
That has entombed this Earth
Far from light or glee.

I feel its ghostly hand
Settle on my beating heart
And fearfully I flee
Retreating to thawing Earth.

Until the dawn has come
To slay this icy night
And break its iron grip
Upon my frozen soul.

Jonathan Sharman (16)
Borden Grammar School

Another Expressionism

It is another dimension, another dream,
You drift off in another land,
There are melting clocks, disfigured faces
Other expressionisms of life and death,
The confusion never stops,
Heart passing, another movement.
Glimpses of colours, something shines through
We are in a different motion, however we have not moved.
There is a beauty of a silent appearance,
But a dark side to a silent emotion.
We look and see history, culture and tradition.
It is right in front of us, a different approach
But why prelude to this dream?
We then see the brush marks and see the talent
And expressionism of every mark made by man.
But can we see different or do we just look and move on?

Natalie Donovan (17)
Borden Grammar School

The Hurricane

I knew it was going to come, I knew it was going to hurt.
It's going to come in a flash, I'd better be alert.

It was getting closer, it was nearly here.
I know that when it hits us, I'm going to shed a tear.

It was right beside me, I could nearly touch it.
The strong winds that it carries, my house is going to be shredded.

It was right on top of me, the buildings were blowing away.
With speeds of 200+mph, I hope it doesn't last all day.

The destruction that it left, will take a decade to fix.
The houses were expensive and now it's all in a mix.

The tides first started to rise, it then began to rain.
With storms in front and behind it, I knew it was a hurricane.

Dean Brown (13)
Borden Grammar School

The End

They sit you in a small, uncomfortable chair,
All you can do is think and stare,
Feeling very isolated,
Look at your pen - all masticated.
There is no other option now,
You can't get up and walk out,
At nine o'clock it finally starts,
You feel your chest, your heart beats fast.
Several thoughts run through your head,
You wish it was seven and you were still in bed,
At last you pick up your pen,
But now, where to begin?
Half an hour has passed,
You better start working fast,
As you watch time fly,
Several people walk up and down, passing by.
As the clock strikes half-ten,
Put down your pen,
It's all over, this is the end!

Harrison Fry (16)
Borden Grammar School

The Eye Of The Tiger

He waited to enter the huge, colossal coliseum,
Stomachs churning with butterflies whizzing about,
The gladiator departs into the stadium,
Crowds roar at the powerful, bold men,
The opponent, fierce as a tiger in a cage, waiting to pounce,
Both teams standing, staring into the eyes of the prey,
It all kicks off, giant men racing towards each other,
Bodies bruised and battered in this dangerous sport,
They fight for a long eighty minutes, tired and sick,
The men score, level on points and ready to kick,
The conversion is scored, the Twickenham crowd roars,
Gladiators victorious as they win the rugby world cup.

David Walker (14)
Borden Grammar School

Cassiopeia

All I have left;
are pictures and scars and dreams to hold on to;
I'll never wish on that star again.
But, you are the brightest light,
in that pocketful of skies.
The time is 2.22
and I hope your wish comes true
you say I'll know before you do
I hope you're right.
Why can we talk this way?
Being so far away; sitting here.
It's 10.00 your time, 1.00 by mine
often wondering why we met here
the time is 2.22
and I hope my wish comes true
I think I'll know just when you do
I hope I do.
Maybe this is just what I need
maybe I'm wrong
but, unlike mine and me
her picture will remain unbroken
as she calls out,
'Tonight, I fall in love.'
. . . Here's our hands against our hearts.

James Forster (16)
Borden Grammar School

Work!

Work is a task that schools must do,
They say it's just to pull you through,
They say it's for the best of you,
They teach you stuff like statistics
And I don't understand logistics.

Work is something engineers must do,
To get all the men through,
To get them back to wives and families,
Building bridges whilst returning fire
And would you believe they know logistics.

Work is something pilots must do,
To get all the passengers to
The places they ask to go,
They do it as fast as possible,
It's all to do with statistics.

James Herbert (14)
Borden Grammar School

The Last Movement

A soldier who stands is a valiant soldier
But the chances are he'll end up lifeless
A soldier is a persistent soldier
But most soldiers are clueless

In the First World War
England had 100,000 experienced soldiers
But that was not enough to draw
With the German machine guns

A trench in the war
Was sliming with mud
But for food there was no boar
But rations or bread was all they had.

Patrick Smith (13)
Borden Grammar School

Isn't It Ironic?

The sun is setting in the east
And the Redwings return home once more.
A bleak, black cloud is now gathering
Over the lands that I yearn to discover,
Before their mystery is spent.

But I cannot, tho' while my body is but ashes,
My will is ablaze.
While the shadow of death stalks me,
I am ever one step ahead
And while I am an old man
And people have written me off
I say, 'All aboard.'

No my friends, these are false, tho' wish were true
For it brings grievances to my soul, knowing
That the mere swaying of a vessel upon a wave
Brings ailment to my stomach, and
Nausea to my mind.
Please, please tell me;
How could it ever come down to this?

Chris McGee (16)
Borden Grammar School

Basketball

As you fly up the court
You remember the battle that you fought
With your weapon in your hand
You run across the guarded land
You spring and pounce, you jump and roll
As you head towards your goal
You finally reach your destination
You settle in your firing station
You go to make your final shot
You've trained so hard and tried a lot
You shoot the ball and it goes in
The match is over, your team win.

Ben Comery (14)
Borden Grammar School

Two Catholic Leprechauns Playing Poker In My Bath

Two Catholic leprechauns playing poker in my bath,
One named Jeremiah the other named Mark,
Jeremiah worked in a pharmacy in Bristol,
Mark was fully qualified, full-time flower arranger (but he never
                                                                   bragged),
They had met on an exotic cruise round the Caribbean,
Jeremiah was visiting his mother-in-law the mermaid,
She had tried to eat Mark and Jeremiah had convinced her not to
                                                                    (well, that's what he said).

Well that's fair enough, I thought,
But why are there two ginger midgets playing poker in my bath?
'Well it seemed like a good place at the time,' said Mark,
'Yes, and I do like what you've done with the tiles.'
'I don't really have time to talk,' I said,
'I really need to use the toilet.'
'Don't worry,' said Jeremiah,
'I won't look.'

They carried on playing,
I got quite mad,
Things were heating up,
It got pretty bad,
'I'm sorry but I really need you to leave.'
And so they did, *pop,*
That was it,
The end.

James Cross (13)
Borden Grammar School

Cars

Cars line up,
Ready to race,
The drivers look at each other,
Face to face

The music blaring,
All the cars tuned
Get caught by the police
And you are doomed!

Now racing,
Weaving traffic,
The slightest mistake,
Could be tragic.

Side by side,
All the way
If you lose the race,
Then you will pay

Speeding up,
Finish line near
The police then came
They rode with fear . . .

Michael Baxendale (15)
Borden Grammar School

Eyes

My eyes burn,
My eyes burn with anger.
I can feel the steam rising in my eyes,
It glows red in revenge.
I can feel the scorching heat in the air,
The anger can't be stopped,
It's in control!
My eyes are ready to explode,
To release the persisting fire,
Fury will unleash!

Simon Cuthbert (13)
Borden Grammar School

The Goal

Standing waiting to kick off,
As the referee prepares his watch,
You can feel the pressure,
Building in your stomach,
Speed is vital to win the ball,
You've won the ball, now your skill will show,
Those hours of practise have paid off,
You knock the ball around the opposing player,
You will now show your fitness to get there first,
You're successful, you get there before,
Now keep your composure,
Use your quality,
You've placed the ball into the top corner with accuracy,
An amazing finish,
To an incredible move,
Goal!

Callum Essam (13)
Borden Grammar School

The Wonderful Waterfall

Water flowing down
Crash, crash, crash as the water hits the ground
Foam bubbling by the rocks
The ear-splitting sound it makes

The water screaming down
The wetness in the air
The rocks shining in the light
What was once silence in the air,
Is now a deafening sound.

People looking with amaze
They say it is like a TV with no signal
The water gushing through this maze
That is the wonderful waterfall.

Johnathan Rudland (13)
Borden Grammar School

The Grandfather Clock

The authentic grandfather clock sits there,
At all the hours of the day,
With many cobwebs brushed away,
The sharp clicking every second,
Warn people of its whereabouts,
The smooth carvings of the wood,
Shows the skilful hands under the hood,

A forbidden house is where it stands,
The door is put on lock,
The soft chime of the clock,
The hands stay sturdy,
In the clock face,
One, long like an aerial,
The other short and stubby

But still the authentic grandfather clock
Sits there waiting.

Jordan Ingram (13)
Borden Grammar School

Autumn

Autumn winds swirling leaves,
To the ground,
Without a sound,
Cascades of red and gold,
A sight to behold.

The crazy, hazy sunshine,
Of the afternoon,
Makes a riot of colour,
In borders and shrubs,
With bonfires burning,
To end this delightful season.

Samuel Williamson (13)
Borden Grammar School

The Pianist

Sliding across the slippery keys,
Walking fingers,
Black and white is all I see,
Walking fingers,
Strutting up and down again,
Walking fingers,
Rushing like a speeding train,
Walking fingers.

Fingers are swans gliding gracefully,
Making music,
Fingers like tigers pouncing stealthily,
Making music,
Fingers are spiders tiptoeing softly,
Making music,
Fingers like elephants trampling loudly,
Making music.

From deep inside the dusty darkness,
Sounds are coming,
Notes emerging through the calmness,
Sounds are coming,
Chords and melodies spiralling high,
Sounds are coming,
A hail of composition flashes by,
Sounds have gone.

Richard Moakes (13)
Borden Grammar School

The Three Soldiers

The torn ground presents pathways,
That the soldiers creep through,
The ground below is barren and fragmented.
Under the surface, tissue and bones lay in wait.
Full of bravery the soldiers poise.
Ready for the signal. They wait . . .
Finally the signal is given and . . .
Bang! Bang! Bang!
The men fall to the ground.
The heavy winds waft the earth,
Over the wounds of the defunct.
After the battleground is fled,
A brief ceremony is held for the three soldiers, dead.

Andrew Walker (13)
Borden Grammar School

The Coming

I hear the roar
And the banging on my door
It's coming, it's coming
The rattle on the ground,
Can be heard all around
It's coming, it's coming
The face the colour of gold
It has turned really cold
It's coming, it's coming
He has caught me with his teeth
I turned in disbelief
It has come, it has come!

James Bowen (13)
Borden Grammar School

The Second Earth

As I peacefully float over the warmth of the Mediterranean
I roll over and what do I see
A crab scuttling on the seabed, side to side, not like you and me
I hold my breath and take a dive.
I spot a turtle lumbering past, slower on land than in sea.
I see plant life swaying in the currents of the ocean.
Then, suddenly, I'm being dragged along, the current's got me
I try to swim away, but the power is overwhelming
It's like I'm a particle of dust and a Hoover's sucked me in
Then, the current has had enough of me and hurls me out.
Above me I see one of the most spectacular living creatures.
A blue whale, its tail forcefully propelling it to the surface for air
It jumps swallowing litres of air, its tail creating a mighty splash
It should be good for another hour or two
As it dives back down it spots me and begins to open its mouth
Oh no, it's going to swallow me and then I start panicking
As it approaches it picks up pace
I scream only letting out air bubbles, then faint.

Robert Burton (13)
Borden Grammar School

The Gentle Killer

Slowly the engine begins to purr,
Its smoothly crafted, shiny brown body begins to vibrate softly,
The burnt rubber on the wheels prepares itself for another pounding.
Swoosh, swoosh, the three bit propeller begins to spin,
The bright and wonderful piece of ingenuity begins to roll along,
then it turns to a jog
and then a gallop and . . . and it's flying.
You can see the air being slipstreamed along the streamlined body,
the Spitfire's safety catch is off.
This incredible work of art has turned from a baby hippopotamus
to a fully-grown adult; it is a killing machine.

Patrick Hall (13)
Borden Grammar School

The Baseball

When you hold it in your hand,
You're in the middle of a stand,
With the skill that's involved,
Forces it to revolve.

Expelled with phenomenal power,
Which would reach to the highest of towers,
The accuracy and speed,
To ensure all take heed.

The spherical shape,
Makes everyone gape,
Piercing through the air,
Knowing everyone's aware.

We've won!

Tom Woolnough (14)
Borden Grammar School

The Mountain

The
mountain,
brutal, cold
and dangerous. The
mountain is something
to be afraid of. There is a
chance of death to whoever is
on its face, the trees shake with fear
as a cloud of snow and ice come tumbling
down the mountain. Whomever on its face brings
to crumble. You are frozen with fear, but there is another
side of the mountain, sunny and playful, it is a picturesque side,
a beautiful wondrous place, but the monster is not to be forgotten.

Matthew Jordan (14)
Borden Grammar School

Them

The soft, silk-like feeling
Underneath the hard above
They have had a lot of pain
A giant ball is its enemy
It blocks the fortress over and over
Until the fight is won
It can grip and catch the enemy
Throwing it and kicking it
As the enemy attacks
The fortress would lose all
If they were not there
They can pounce and attack
Using both the hard and soft sides
There are so many different types
But only one pair is needed
They are the saviours
Of every squad
Every goalkeeper has them
Goalkeeper gloves.

George Packer (14)
Borden Grammar School

The Guitar

The assassin walks forward,
Wielding his chosen weapon of audio assault.
He takes his first shot,
It sounds like a squealing cat.

He gets to the ensemble of the onslaught,
Caning the six triggers of sound.
Shooting projectile soundwaves,
That bounce back from the victims.

The squealing cat returns,
Suddenly the cat is abruptly killed.
The guitar becomes lifeless,
The audience roar at the performance.

Sam Duchesne (12)
Borden Grammar School

Sunny Lane

As I walked down sunny lane
A sudden thought rushed to my brain
If I could sail the seven seas
It may just help me find the keys
To unlock my hidden life
Oh how I pray for kids and wife
I want to bring life to this land
So I can find my hidden man
This is my one and single desire
Burning bright like love's great fire
I never want these days to end
A family man's my chosen trend
I love these kids like God loves all
For them I'd climb a mountain tall
I'd give my life for them to be
For I trust God to protect me.

Daniel Campbell (14)
Borden Grammar School

What Am I?

What am I?
Slithering through the grass
Sensing my destination
Seeking a rock for shelter
Trying to avoid the rays of sunlight
Waiting for darkness to fall upon me.
Hunger strikes
Searching for my food
Moonlight shining onto my fangs
Waiting, waiting, waiting
I pounce, my hunger is taken away
I sense footsteps
I get more and more nervous
I rattle
What am I?

Michael Phillips (14)
Borden Grammar School

The Salmon

Look at that salmon swimming upstream,
He must know that's an impossible dream.
Don't you think he gets worn out?
I think so, without a doubt!
All its life it pushes and swims,
How it must ache his little fins.
Look, he's coming up to a waterfall,
If he makes it up, that would be so cool!
Go on my son, you can do it,
He's fallen down, now he's blown it!
Wow! He's just made it up the waterfall,
Oh look, he's just so small,
You mean compared to that grizzly bear,
I wonder if he can get out of there?
His teeth are like a set of daggers,
Now I bet that's he's cream-crackered!

Stuart Brown (14)
Borden Grammar School

A Salmon's Dream

A salmon's dream
Is to swim upstream
He must know it is an impossible dream
Like pigs flying and houses underwater
But he keeps trying, he won't give up
He'll keep trying until his luck is up
But until that day he'll keep swimming
Thinking of the dream that he's missing
Trying harder and harder to complete his goal
Until one day he's grey and old
Hoping his son will complete his dream
And all salmon will swim upstream.

Laurence Billing (14)
Borden Grammar School

Warriors

As the gladiators parade out in a orderly fashion,
Looking at the enemy as placid as a tree stump,
Ready to pounce on the bulls,
He leaps forward looking like a cheetah,
Chasing and chasing the beasts with a force.

Sweating all over trying his best,
Grabbing the rope, swinging and swinging
Forcing the great bulls back,
Effective dodging is the key,
Teasing them until they wear out.

Finally he's near, but a trip causes a smash on the ground
Standing up and cheering
The crowd alight
Who is this?

It's Jonny Wilkinson scoring another try
Against the Bradford Bulls.

Gareth Messenger (12)
Borden Grammar School

The Dark Green Car

It stands there on the field looking *so* immaculate
It has clean white hubs and a dark green body
When it starts it moans and groans as if it's talking to you
It enters the woodland and as it disappears it reflects a sparkle of sun
As it goes round it bumps and scrapes the trees and the ground
It goes down into a ditch full of mud and gets caked in the mud
It looks all dull in the middle of the woods
When it comes out it is not clean, the white hubs are now brown
It stops with mud dropping onto the open field
It is now standing there, silent with mud splashes all over it
It is a car, a dark green Land Rover
Not only is it a Land Rover, it is my Land Rover in Land Rover green.

Jack Mundy (14)
Borden Grammar School

As The Train Goes By

Every day the train goes by,
Always five minutes late,
I hear the clickety-clack,
The engines roaring,
I look inside at the screaming babies,
Their mothers in hysterics,
The business men are all the same,
Reading the paper or solemnly looking at a laptop,
Mobiles ringing,
Wives asking if the train is on time,
The driver sits at the front,
He just wants to go home,
But I'm afraid not,
There are many more trips to be made,
And now . . . it is gone!

Ben Lane (12)
Borden Grammar School

Poem Of A Warrior

He surveys the scene,
Ever wary of every movement.
A determined frown set upon his handsome countenance.
His hand rests upon the hilt of his trusty blade.
His cloak billows out behind him,
His long fair hair flying.
At last he is rewarded for his patient waiting.
The glint of the sun's rays on armour!
The enemy is nigh!
Slowly, calmly, he unsheathes his sword.
Alone,
Standing against impossible odds,
No more frightened than a child of a pet.
That is the way of the warrior.

Sam Thomas (12)
Borden Grammar School

The Final

This was it, the final!
My stomach crumbled,
like soil in your hand.
My legs wobbled,
like jelly on a plate.
My hands trembled,
like an earthquake.
My heart thumped,
like the drums.
Bang!
I was off,
like a rocket.
I was gliding through the air,
like a bird.
I was cruising to victory,
like a true champion.
When?

Ryan Rook (14)
Borden Grammar School

The Wicket

I'm working out my run up,
Where should I pitch the ball,
Where? Where? Over there, over there,
I know where.

I start to run,
I jump and release the ball,
It hurtles through the air,
It bounces.

And then,
It goes through the batsman,
It hits the stump,
Howzat!

Nathan Foster (12)
Borden Grammar School

The Boy Who Was Foolish

Now there once was a boy,
So young and so foolish,
He committed a crime,
For being so fiendish.

He went to court,
And got a decision,
Jail, or a magnificent camp,
For boys in his position!

Well I will choose camp!
Hooray! He thought,
Now I can fly,
So gloriously in the sky!

Now there once was,
A very, unlucky boy,
Now in a field, picking berries,
Thinking of miraculous fairies . . .

That will whisk him away,
To make a decision,
And this time he'll choose . . .
Prison!

Declan Cornelius (12)
Borden Grammar School

The Cheetah

The almighty cheetah runs for its prey
The gazelle is the prey,
Trying to escape the fear,
As the predator's legs pump out of the blocks,
The prey's petrified skeleton shakes
And he beams with pride,
It's slender body powerful and rapid,
As the carcass isn't there for long,
As he shows how mighty he is,
As he lifts his trophy.

Liam Ward (12)
Borden Grammar School

The Times Past

Trees swaying in the breeze,
Each leaf swinging and swaying,
Rejected leaves from seasons past,
Rustling noisily on the grass,
Seasons gone, moving on,
Twinkling dew drops on the grass,
Children playing in the snow,
Animals sleeping, lying low,
Children sitting on Santa's knee,
Asking for presents from him and thee,
Seasons gone, moving on,
The year is young,
New buds have sprung,
Reaching out towards the sun,
Flowers blossom in a pungent flourish,
Seasons gone, moving on,
The sun is hot,
The sky is bright,
The moon doesn't appear until late at night,
Children playing and having fun,
Beneath the radiator we call the sun!

Lee Rogers (12)
Borden Grammar School

The Journey Of An Oak

I fall out of the sky, thud!
On the earth I burrowed down.
My legs descend, my arms held high above
My fingers feeling for the light
To give me a thought to grow.
My waistline thickens year by year
As I age, my joints begin to knarl.
Now I am old and start to rot
I know my end, thud!

By A N Oak.

Christopher Jenkins (13)
Borden Grammar School

Success

He marks out his run.
Where, what, why?
Where shall I put this ball?
What will I bowl?
Why will I do that?
He asks himself.
He walks up, all eyes on him.
He bowls the ball.
It is a swirling mass fizzing through the air.
It bounces
It spits and rips off the surface
A solid wooden stick swung past it.
It did not connect.
It hits the goal.
The stumps cartwheel elegantly through the air.
Success!

Dominic Campbell (12)
Borden Grammar School

Lead Into War

I bravely stride into the battle-ridden war zone,
My gun is clenched tightly in my hand.
Bang! A bullet flies past my face.
Missing me by a millimetre.
I start to run as fast as I can,
The bullets barely missing me, yet again.
I turn to fire my gun at the origin of the bullets,
But by the time I turned round I felt an intense pain,
On my side
I fell to the floor in agony,
I watched the red liquid flow down my body!
I tried to get up but the pain was too unbearable,
The paint ball had hit me too hard to get up!
I crawled to the sideline and laid down until the next round . . .

Ahmet Eken (12)
Borden Grammar School

The Striker

He's coming,
Like a train on a track,
Driving his way through
Every piece of grass in his way.
He's coming,
Like a madman on the loose
Getting closer and closer
To glory.
He shoots,
And the ball travels
Like a rocket through the air.
The keeper dives,
Hoping to keep his team in the game.
But he doesn't.
He's already celebrating
Before the ball's in the net.
A true striker.

Liam O'Donoghue (12)
Borden Grammar School

The Wood Beams

If only, if only the wood beams sigh,
If only I had a pair of eyes,
To tell you all the sights I've seen,
To clear up history and clear up lies.

If only, if only the wood beams sigh,
I could tell you of all the tales
The tales of old and parliament's lies,
The truth of Henry VIII and all his wives.

If only, if only the wood beams sigh,
If only I could have a pair of eyes,
To tell the truth and all the lies,
If only, if only the wood beams cry.

Matthew Ingram (12)
Borden Grammar School

Poem

Just a curb, but the curb I must jump,
A wall blocking my path to glory.
I set off skating as fast as I can
The wind whipping through my hair.

I descend down the hill, my pace quickens
My legs tense with anticipation,
My feet shift to a better position,
As the curb comes closer, closer, closer.

Suddenly the curb is upon me
When should I kick, so hard to judge,
But my legs cannot stay coiled anymore,
My legs let loose, any energy is pulled upwards.

The wood slaps the pavement floor
As I take to the air, momentarily
And as instinct almost tells me to
I slam all four wheels to the path
My goal has been reached and well deserved.

Patrick Collins (12)
Borden Grammar School

Battlefield!

I am a centurion,
Strong, brave and fearless.
I lead out my men onto the battlefield,
We shall be fighting
Our worst, dreaded, opposing enemies.
We have trained hard,
Our tactical movement has been practised to perfection.
The defence tactics we use are very effective.
They make their first move,
Then we make ours.
We are about to attack
Then I strike.
Goal!

Luke Bowerman (12)
Borden Grammar School

The Blue Yonder

The blue yonder of the sea,
What memories it holds for me,
The crashing waves of the night,
As a child I knew no spite.
It used to keep me up all night long,
Like a nightingale singing an everlasting song.

I used to wonder what was there,
I used to stop and stand and stare,
I used to have not a single care,
I used to watch it tear the beach
And gazed beneath its blue sheath,
The mainland though was out of reach.

Eventually, the land would keel,
To the sea's almighty heel.
It keeps on kicking all the time,
This personality has no mime.

As the boats bob up and down,
I'd often stare and sometimes frown.
As he heads back out to sea,
With a smile upon his face has he.

He knows what lies in the 'blue yonder' of the sea.

Ben Nappey (13)
Borden Grammar School

Rhyme

Rhyme,
What a wonderful word
It sounds
Just like the song of a bird.

Rhyme,
It's what makes two words alike
But
May differ at first sight.

Rhyme,
What an extraordinary thing
Because
It consists of no vowels within.

Rhyme,
In my opinion the best
Verb
Of all the rest.

Rhyme,
It is so unique
It takes
Its meaning to its peak.

You always
Know it's time
When
To start to rhyme.

Michael Friar (12)
Borden Grammar School

Autumn

Days seem shorter
Nights are longer
Winds whispering through the breeze.
Puddles forming
Rainfall daunting
Low sun dazzling onto screens.

Squirrels hibernating
Birds migrating
Flowers losing their will to live.
High tides
Misty hillsides
Trees transparent on landscape scenes.

Hedgehogs rolling
Leaves falling
Brooms sweeping up the path.
Thermal clothing
North winds blowing
Umbrellas turning inside-out.

Red rosy apples
Crisp, hard pears
Cascading in the midnight air.
Pumpkins growing
Candles glowing
Harvest glory produced with care.

Chimneys smoking
Fires choking
Hot soup bubbling on the hearth.
Apple bobbing
Hallowe'en knocking
Autumn brings lots of cheer.

Luke Grubb (12)
Borden Grammar School

Lion Feast

Hungry lion laying suspiciously in long grass
Unsuspecting zebras walking slowly past
Not realising the danger that lurks near
The young and playful, no need to fear.

Starving lion silently waits
Young zebras bolder, unaware of their fate
Inches closer to the unwarned prey
A perfect feast, no time to delay.

Ravenous lion primed to strike
Bewildered zebra unable to fight
Abandoned victim, beautiful prize
Will never again see the sun rise.

Bloated lion, contented beast
Lays beside the mutilated feast
No more killing, at least for today
A brutal existence, but no other way.

Will Halls (12)
Borden Grammar School

Angels Dressed In White

As I was dreaming one night,
I saw angels dressed in white.
Flying slowly through the air,
The angels were saying a prayer.
Bless this one dear Lord,
One day she will get her reward.
She will receive her angel wings,
And join us as we sing.
She will be a strong one you see,
With her wings she will be free.
To find the one who needs her most,
This new angel will stay very close.
To help and guide them through,
Could this angel be for you?

Vindhya Parasher (13)
Bradbourne School

White

White is a star,
That shines so bright.
White is snowballs,
Just right for fights.

White is mountains,
That rid the gloom.
White is lilies,
Starting to bloom.

White is a cloud,
High in the sky.
White is sugar,
Great in a pie.

White is washing,
Out on the line.
White is daisies,
Petals so fine.

White is crushed ice,
It calms the strife.
White is so pure,
It lights up life.

Rebecca Nicholls (13)
Bradbourne School

Reminder: A Bit Close To Home

A burden lingers,
Thee seeks solitude,
But every corner one turns one is reminded.

Shadows gather,
Reality no longer exists,
Trying to escape, trying to be free.

Nicola Smith (13)
Bradbourne School

24 Hooves, 12 Boots

24 hooves thundering in the night
Barely daring to look in fright
24 hooves come to a close
Barely daring to move your pose.

12 boots on the grass
Watch in fear as your partners gasp.
Doors slammed shut
Bolted and locked.
Hear the pistol being fired
For those unlucky enough.

12 boots going back
24 hooves thundering
Back into the night
We're the lucky ones
But there's always tomorrow night . . .

Eloise Macdonald-Meyer (11)
Bradbourne School

Little Butterfly

Little butterfly
fly light in the sky
along with the dragonflies.

Fly down to the old log
see all the little frogs
hopping away from the fat dog.

Little butterfly
you're very tired
fly back to your nettle leaf
and go straight to sleep.

Faye Purchase (11)
Bradbourne School

Mondays

This morning when I got out of bed
I felt a drip, drop on my head
I looked out of my window to see,
It pouring down so heavily.

Oh great! I thought. *A Monday morning
How will I get there when it is pouring?*
But this was not an ordinary day
So weird and strange, normal, no way.

So, on the way to the bus stop
I felt another almighty drop
I ran to shelter under a tree
But with that the sun came out happily.

As soon as I went on my way
It started to pour down again
How weird, I thought *I must be dreaming*
But the sky was absolutely bleeding.

So back I went under a tree
When the sun came out annoyingly
That's it, I stormed, no more games
I don't care if it rains . . .

And then it clicked, hip, hip hooray!
Back to bed I went, it was Sunday!

Chloë Robinson (13)
Bradbourne School

The Girl In The Mirror

I meet the girl in the mirror everyday at half-past seven.
The girl that looks back has blue eyes and is eleven.
She combs her hair when I comb mine
That girl looking back is pretty fine
She could be my twin sister if she wanted to be,
Because the girl in the mirror is me!

Danielle Pyrah (11)
Bradbourne School

Me

I acted as a bridesmaid when I was only two
Dressed in all my finery I made my first debut
At three years old I 'wowed' them as I danced upon the stage
As a bunny I was very cute, the ears were all the rage
It wasn't too long after I rode on a pony's back
But to my disappointment I was far too young to hack
I started in reception class and I could not read and write
Along with all the rest of the class I soon could see the light
I remember - it was book week - and I went in Pinocchio guise
The costume wasn't very good, I didn't win a prize
Sport's Day was very special, I found it so much fun
Everybody cheering as I did my fastest run
In athletics I was chosen to do the javelin throw
Again spectators at the side called, 'Where did that one go?'
School journey was another first, this time away from home
Then of course millennium year I visited The Dome.
So far I have dreams unfulfilled, there's lots I want to do
I realise I'm lucky but I appreciate it too.

Lizzie Hasler (13)
Bradbourne School

Heaven

He walks through the bleak, lonely streets
With rags for his clothes, and blistered, bare feet
With no one to care for and no one to love
His thoughts and prayers heard above
Finally he settles down for the night
But doesn't know that when it turns light
He'll head on to Heaven above,
And when up there, be able to love
Be able to smile, live in comfort and peace,
This night will not be a normal night's sleep
Tired, cold, hungry and unaware,
That he has just uttered his final, last prayer.

Justine Fedorowycz (13)
Bradbourne School

The Snowflake

Catch a falling snowflake, and don't let it melt,
for it is the magic that you have lost, and not dealt,
the magic in the snowflake is not as precious as a star,
but it is still as good so far.
A snowflake so crystal-like,
as pretty as its wake,
just as pretty as a diamond but not the same make.
And in winter, under a thick blanket of snow,
the trees so bare, standing tall,
a pretty sight so nice,
and snowflakes that are falling are upon the ice.

Hayley Dean (11)
Bradbourne School

A Winter's Tale

The pale white duvet of glistening snow
Covers the fresh dew-dripped grass
As winter returns this year.
She has been locked away for three continuing seasons
And is desperate to spread her ivory blanket over the lurking land
Night falls and she swiftly swoops
Her ebony-coloured cloak across the blue skies
And turns it into a star sprinkled, moonlit night.

Lily Fleet-Newman (11)
Bradbourne School

Untitled

Have you ever seen me looking from afar,
I'm often right behind you, when you're driving in your car,
I'd like to flash my lights, and make myself known,
But whenever I'm behind you, you never are alone,
I'd like to get to meet you, I'm sure we'd get on well,
Cos even though we've never met, I think that you're just swell.

Lauren Medhurst (11)
Bradbourne School

Notice

Do they notice
I don't smile and that I'm unhappy?
Do they notice
When I withdraw myself from 'their' world?
Do they notice
When I cry myself to sleep?
Do they notice
All these cuts on my back?
Do they notice
When I don't leave the house for days
Because I'm so low I'm practically on the floor?
Well, do they?

Will they notice
When I don't come home?
Will they notice
When police come to the door to deliver bad news?
Will they notice then?

Will they look at the place where I took my life?
Will they?

Will they cry
That I'm gone?
Will they cry
At how I took my life?
Will they cry
When they are told I'm pregnant?

The answer's no,
They never notice, listen, look or cry
To me or for me and they never will.

Siân Cunningham (13)
Bradbourne School

The Cat No One Wanted

So sleek,
So sly,
So black they all say,
The neighbours gather around,
Dustbins sprawled across the drives
And the vivid, lurching sound.

Petrified, the postman ran
And the panic-stricken child,
They both together saw that cat,
His teeth so sharp and wild.

But alas, one day, we knew it would come,
The cat, he ran astray,
In front of a car, and a big one at that,
Somehow we knew he would pay.

No one loved him, so no one would care,
About that poor little cat,
But I was the one, *I* took him in,
So I thought for a minute, while sat.

Some way we loved him, but shouted we did,
And scolded him more than we may,
But that was the cat that caused all the fuss,
Who sadly passed away!

Laura Sparks (13)
Bradbourne School

Wind

Beware, beware
I can slice you in half,
Grab your leaves with my magical scarf,
I'll snatch your branches
And tear your roots
So beware, beware.

Caris Strain (11)
Bradbourne School

The Sea Is A Swan

                    The sea
                      is a swan
                    that darts
                    through
                      the sand,
                    when I
                    fall
                      over
                      it sprays
                      on my hands
I roll on the sand that sticks to my feet,
   if you listen, the sea makes a beat.
It's time to go now, I've had a good play,
       don't disappear, I'll come
              another day.

Bethany Lynch (11)
Bradbourne School

Earthquake Attack

Tremors shake from the ground,
Everyone is making such a terrible sound,
Buildings are collapsing to the floor,
People are hoping there won't be more,
Destruction is happening through the land,
I need someone to hold my hand,
Many people were killed,
No one's heart will ever be filled,
Dust is spreading all around,
People are hoping to be found,
Everyone's heart starts to race,
Houses are falling out of their place,
Children are getting hit by rubble,
What has caused all this trouble?

Charlotte Farrugia (13)
Bradbourne School

Inside Me . . .

There's a window inside me, shut tightly,
preventing me from bursting into tears.
There's a padlock safe inside me,
keeping my anger locked away.
There's a butterfly inside me, fluttering away
with my dreams on its wings.
There's a marathon runner inside me,
running to my thoughts and imagination.
There's an audience inside me, chanting my name,
waiting for me to get nervous.
There's a book inside me,
waiting for somebody to open it and read my darkest secrets.
There's a rolling pin inside me,
smoothing out my quick and fiery temper.
There's a giraffe inside me,
with all my proudest moments on its long, elegant neck.
There's a trampoline inside me,
waiting for me to jump so high that I would touch the sky.
There's a quilt inside me,
covering someone with a collage of my life so far . . .

Sophie Fordham (11)
Bradbourne School

I Wonder . . .

I love my bear that I cuddle at night
And squeeze so tight
But by day it sits there upon my bed
Looking sad and glum
That I'm not there
Squeezing tight.
She is happy when I'm around.
At school I wonder if she's alright
And wonder if she has a life.
   I wonder!
   I wonder!

Vanessa Gbadebo (11)
Bradbourne School

The Cat

Silently it crept on by
Looking like an evil spy

I felt a sudden rush of air
The cat gave me an evil stare

The cold wind rushed past
Disappearing fast

The cats glowing yellow eyes
Looked at me as it walked on by

Down the street the trees swayed
The cat looked out to catch its prey

All I could see was its swishing tail
Swaying around us slow as a snail

The cat wandered down the street
Dragging along its black feline feet.

Kelly Bryant (13)
Bradbourne School

Jostling Journey

Surreptitious, sleek and swift,
precious as a Heaven gift.
Never pausing as it flows,
passing by peaceful meadows.
Beneath the surface, a village of fish,
darting freely as they wish.
Bubble ripples, rushing waves,
pebbles grow to proud caves.
Curving, colliding, free as life,
an energetic force that's never in strife.
Surreptitious, sleek and swift,
pure as a Heaven gift.

Ellen Tout (13)
Bradbourne School

Tropical Fish

As I sat proud, gazing into my beautifully decorated fish tank,
I watched with interest, the sleek fish swim by.

A spectrum of colours gliding smoothly
through the fresh, clear water,
dashing quickly to get their food.

Pearlised patterns and stunning, shiny speckles.
Transparent fins and delicate tails,
swishing through the crystal water.

The glass surface reflecting the bright beams of sunlight.
Nothing better than to have
this outstanding tropical fish tank in your sight.

Fish resting in-between the plantations,
disguising themselves in the tall, swaying reeds.

Wiggling weeds waving in the water, grass and anemones,
the best place to hide in a game of hide-and-seek.

Kayleigh Jarrett (13)
Bradbourne School

Why Is The Nation So Dirty?

Crisp packets flying in the wind,
Empty bottles thrown in hedges,
Chocolate wrappers, overflowing bins!

Why is the nation so dirty?

Chewing gum spat onto paths,
Glass is scattered over roads,
People litter and start to laugh!

Why is the nation so dirty?

Bianca Lefevre (11)
Bradbourne School

Good And Bad

I am the good,
I am the bad,
I feel happy,
I feel sad,
I use pink and blue fluffy clouds,
I choose darkened, black, misty shrouds,
I like glistening, shiny fairy dust,
I like heartless, brutal hate and lust,
A beauty princess in her glory,
A wicked witch who's very gory,
A tall castle stood on the hill,
An inspirational dungeon death fulfil.
Sweet ab-fab kitten in the flowers,
Big black cat among rain showers,
Little butterfly flying round,
Dead black bat upon the ground,
Sunshine shining in the sky,
The demon child lets out a cry,
I made the happy,
I made the sad,
I come from Heaven,
I come from Hell,
I keep all secrets,
I always tell,
I'll call the angels we will win,
I'll call the undead they will begin,
I'll rise above you with the love,
I'll call the lightning from above,
I am good I'll always win,
Because I never ever, ever sin.

Tina Smith-Reeve (13)
Bradbourne School

A Summer's Day

The summer's sun and shade,
The rippled water to wade.
The summer's trees swayed,
On the flower beds I laid.
The summer's slimy bugs,
Crawled beneath the grass like rugs.
The summer's tomatoes and corn,
Its dew in the morn.
The summer's scented flowers,
Bow over me like towers.
The summer's sandy beaches,
The cherries and juicy peaches.
The summer's girls and boys,
The air full of lots of noise.
The summer's clouds in the sky,
Hot whipped cream on a pie.
The summer's honeybees
Are a delight for me to see.
The summer's ice cream
Filled with joy just like dreams
The summer's sand,
To lay on to get a tan.
The summer's fun,
To play in the park in the sun.
The summer's time to swim, splash and fish,
And to go on a picnic if you wish.
The summer's vacation,
There never is a complication.
The summer's hot sunny sky,
It's summer, that's why!
I love summer!

Becky Bailey (13)
Bradbourne School

Merlin

My dog Merlin is a Great Dane,
Sometimes he can be a great pain,
He woofs to go out and knocks to come in,
And when you're not looking he goes through the bin,
He scares all my friends with a big, friendly lick
And sometimes their sweets he will sneak up and nick.
He's big, grey, with big black spots,
He's my dog Merlin and I love him lots.

Jessika Cruse (11)
Bradbourne School

My Perfect Dream

The glittery star twinkles in the night light.
The moon, beautiful mirror, swimming in milky cloud.
Breeze like love dancing in soft, slow summer sky.
Old wise bird only sounds lazy, great triumph.
I will be above it all in Heaven.

Natasha Bray (11)
Bradbourne School

Fears

The creaking of the stairs in the dead of night,
Only darkness and silence, no light.
The moon like a giant's gleaming eye,
Unblinking, penetrating. Why?

Slowly, I started to doze . . .
I heard a noise, and froze,
'It's nothing,' I said, nothing there at all.
I lay back down, and I slept.
Peaceful and calm not a noise at all.
I thought to myself . . . *what a fool.*

Nic Taylor (12)
Dorton House School For The Blind

Amersham

My room downstairs.
Guess what it's got?
A tracking hoist like an arm,
Holding me.
A great bed, with a white bed head
And sides protecting me.
Two shelves for books,
Wooden wardrobe,
And a CD player
Winding down.

I chose the colour myself, you know?
Lilac walls.
Carpet cushioning me,
Blue curtains opening up the sun.
At home,
In Amersham.

Kirsten Read (15)
Dorton House School For The Blind

The Wedding

Brilliant silver rings
Exchanging.
Wonderful wedding cotton clothes.
Long white sharvanies down to the floor.
Spectacular food,
Feasting.
Fizzy, dizzy drink.

Rose-red tablecloths,
Drumming Indian music charming ears.
Happy bride laughing,
Groom dancing,
Friends chatting,
Customs creating,
Traditions,
A memorable day.

Abdul Hameed (15)
Dorton House School For The Blind

Lords

Solid wooden bat,
The smooth green grass,
The hard swing ball,
Whacked on the padded gloves,
The wide black sidescreen,
Gliding sideways across the tracks,
White clothed umpires telling, explaining, deciding.
Pubs in the cricket clubs noisy, smoky,
Excited crowd shouting, dancing,
Changing room showers clean and tidy,
Scoreboard informing the crowds.

My dad and I
Going home
Very excited,
Over the moon,
Our day at the cricket,
Superb!

Hammad Husain (15)
Dorton House School For The Blind

Hamster

He is asleep in his cage,
Dreaming about me today.
Dreaming to be free.
Dreaming of his tea?
I will feed him when I get in.
In his cage on the table.
He misses me when I am not there
And I miss him when I'm not there.
He feels soft in my hand,
Cute and cuddle,
Warm and snugly.
A friend, my friend,
I will love him
To the end.

Emma Galvin (15)
Dorton House School For The Blind

At Dad's

On Friday
Arrive at Dad's.
'Let's go out to Nan's.'
'Mmmm!' Dinner . . .

Helplessly hungry.
Gorgeous smells,
Mumbling
From the kitchen.
'Just coming!'
Patience demanding attention.
At last
Satisfied.

Pyjama party,
Relaxed,
Wearing pyjamas all day,
Watching 'telly' together,
EastEnders,
Dramatic disasters,
Crafty characters,
Episodes exploding.
Waiting anxiously
What's going to happen
Next week with Dad?

Charlotte Davey-Whiting (13)
Dorton House School For The Blind

ICT

Computer monitor,
Mouse moving around,
Click on icons,
Speech software,
Headphones, hearing a voice
In your head.
Connections connecting cables,
Like laces.
CD ROM tracks round,
Spinning like a roundabout
Playing games.
Listen to music
Study, work hard and achieve.
Keyboard tapping desperately.
Copy and paste
Save
'Log off now, please?'
Alt F4, pop up
Menu.
Shut down!
Log off Daniel McGee.

Daniel McGee (14)
Dorton House School For The Blind

Cat

My cat has a pain in his ear
He has not been to the vet in a year.
This will be his first time there
So he will be shaken on a chair.

Daddy will put him in a cat box
And shock his little cotton socks.
I hope the vet says he's OK
So he can go out and play.

Josie Hammond (12)
Dorton House School For The Blind

Lego

Bricks of different sizes,
Connecting colours,
Clicking together.
Massive MDF board
Like a table top
A building site
To work on.
Cable cars carrying crates
Cranes creaking.
Building bricks building high
Feeling happy, feeling high
Low down, break down
Demolish, destroy, destruct
Put it away,
It's time for tea.

James Neate (15)
Dorton House School For The Blind

Waiting For Break Time

English.
Sitting there,
Waiting . . . tapping. Sigh!
Can I get out?
Frustration!
Hard work
Writing,
Reading,
Talking,
Bored!
Listen to the teacher.
'Please sit up straight.'
'Well done!'
'Break time!'

Matthew Cleave (14)
Dorton House School For The Blind

Grooming Shadow

Body brush grooming,
Dusting minute mites,
Dandy brush,
Plastic curry comb,
Saddle soap,
Water bucket,
Tack, bit, girth,
Saddle, reins.

My pony Shadow,
My palomino friend,
'Gorgeous baby girl.'
Brushing, rubbing, combing
Cleaning, washing, stroking
'Precious princess poppet.'
Brown, shiny saddle
Cleaned with saddle soap.
Lovely smell of leather
Lovely smell of soap.
Lovely, happy Shadow.

Lottie Smith (15)
Dorton House School For The Blind

Can Arsenal Win?

Henry to Ljungberg, what a pass
The crowd are watching him go;
Will he score? I hope he does, and yes it's in the net!

What a goal, they don't come better,
The crowd are going berserk,
The players all leap in their delight,
It must have been a record.

Newcastle score, the race is on
Can Arsenal come back?
A minute to go, why are they so slow?
Hang on, *yes, it's two!*

Bradley Pilkington (14)
Dorton House School For The Blind

Video Games

Rushing in from school after a long, hard day,
Sitting down on my warm, comfy chair.
Reaching for the power button while tingling with excitement.
My Xbox console groans into action.

I pick up the controller which is as big as a brick.
I load my game with baited breath.
Wondering what adventures await me.
Can't this machine go any faster?

Will it be combat?
Will it be exploring?
Who knows!
Bingo! The game has loaded!

I yell with excitement as I begin to play.
All of sudden, I am in the game.
Now I am ready for action!

On the screen I see enemies ahead.
I charge forward with weapons drawn.
A battle begins but I hold firm.
While concentrating with all my might.

All of a sudden, is that Mum calling?
Can I keep my enemies stalling?
All of a sudden the game is over.
My anger is beginning to boil over.

I throw my controller down in rage.
Because now I have to start again.
But wait . . .

Jack Blackmore (12)
Dorton House School For The Blind

The Sea

Beach like a field of wheat,
'Sea's calm.'
Sand comfortable and silent,
Waves wishing for sun,
Seagulls flapping,
Bird droppings, white.

Blue sky,
Donkeys walking on the path.
Over the sea.
Wooden floorboards
All in a line.
Busy people playing
Games,
Money,
Crashing cups.

Wooing waves coming onto
The sand.
Music playing
Love songs.
Seaweed, lying,
Lunging lazily.
Hanging out!
Talking children on the path,
Hot dogs cooking
Sunday.
A great day to go.

Christine Payne (14)
Dorton House School For The Blind

The Bus

People crowded
Standing like stairs.
Buggies bulging with
Babies,
Sitting in them like shopping.

Books silent,
Glasses on noses,
Papers rustling on people's laps.

Signs on the walls,
Traffic lights stopping,
Dinging bells,
Doors shutting.

Passes out for the driver,
Cigarettes smoking,
Coughing children,
Coats for the cold,
Apple-red buses.

Hayleigh Rayment (14)
Dorton House School For The Blind

Colours

Red is for danger
You must know when to stop.
Blue is the colour of the sky
Bright and so clear.
Black is a feeling when
Things don't go right.
Yellow is happy
Feeling so light
Green is the colour of peas.

Sam Coomber (12)
Furness Special School

Seasons

Spring
Flowers start to bloom!
Animals start to wake up
Trees grow leaves again

Summer
The sun starts to shine
The weather starts to warm up
I can't go Jostle.

Autumn
The leaves start to fall
Animals go gather food
Then they go to sleep

Winter
It starts to get cold
It is the time to keep warm
Turn the heating on.

James Ruane (12)
Furness Special School

Dream Haiku

Tanned girls are the best
On the beach in Jamaica
We went partying.

Louis Vincent (12)
Furness Special School

Autumn Haiku

Fireworks exploded
Big rabbits ran very fast
Leaves are very nice.

Daniel Taylor (11)
Furness Special School

Balloons And Pelicans At Leeds Castle

A group of brightly coloured hot air balloons slowly migrate south,
While a flock of downy white pelicans,
Eagerly squawk awaiting their turn in the sky.

The castle looks on wistfully,
At the sky-dwellers he would love to join,
Could he fly he would travel the world,
See all the sights, smells and sounds,
But instead he is firmly rooted on the ground,
With the same sights, smells and sounds day after day.

As the bright balloons float off into the distance,
With the pelicans in slow, graceful pursuit,
The castle sighs once more for the life of flight he longs for.

Jennifer Brockwell (12)
Homewood School

The Forest

The waterfall gushed softly
over the mossy rocks.
The water was like liquefied diamonds
shimmering as it went by.

The trees were the towers of old
with servants growing around them
with beautiful hair swaying in the wind,
faithful servants looking after the towers of old.

The smell of the rocks was like breathing in freshness
the big rocks had more plants on them
the small were letting water through
each and every one singing their own individual song.

Sam Boxall (12)
Homewood School

Jungle Tiger In The Night

Raining
   Raining
      Raining
The pitter-pattering of the rain
The lightning strikes against the jungle's pain
It burns the sodden ground
The clouds in the wind go swirling round
The wind making a fowl howling sound.

Cracking
   Creaking
      Breaking
Leaves slapping, trembling in the thrashing wind
Shining the green verdant foliage
Waving in distress.
The frightened creatures flock in fear
To dens and burrows disappear.

Prowling
   Roaring
      Hunting
Stealthily, cunningly, hunting unsuspecting prey.
Bearing shiny white fangs like stars in the pitch-black abyss
Tiger, tiger creeping near, this great cat has no fear.

Robert Button (12)
Homewood School

The Beauteous Day . . .

The rocks old and wise,
hide themselves from the skies,
whilst trickling ice-cold water drives on by over their mossy backs.
Rustling leaves in the breeze
froze upon the buzzing bees.
The smell was overpowering of evergreen and outstanding.
The sound was beauteous of birds, calm and free breath.
Smell the wondrous smell I say.

Mikala Brown (13)
Homewood School

The Liquid Diamond Waterfall

The waterfall wound round the rocks,
Trickling past the croaking frogs.
Then it drops down big drops,
To greet even more messy rocks.
It sees the beauty of the sea,
And pours its power into the unknown.

The rocks, rocks, old and wise,
Hide their secrets from the lies.
Its power, its glory, hidden away,
Never to be seen again.
Like ancient secrets buried deep,
Hiding from death and deceit.

The trees, tall and proud,
Sway in the gentle, chilling breeze.
While listening to the peaceful trickle,
Of the liquid diamond waterfall.

Thomas Bushell (12)
Homewood School

The Sunny Beach

The beaches look gold,
The beaches look rare,
The beaches look gold,
Sitting over there.

The tree looks lonely,
The tree looks bare,
The tree looks lonely,
Standing over there.

The sky looks empty,
The sky looks bare
The sky looks empty,
Lying up there.

Becky Budgen (12)
Homewood School

The Beech Tree

The grand beech tree stood,
Its branches reaching out,
Grasping the air with its witch-like claws.
The golden sunlight caught,
On its golden-brown leaves.

Below stood horses,
Grazing in the fresh, dewy grass,
Their tails swishing away flies,
Glinting in the sunlight.

And along the dusty track,
Walked a donkey, pulling a cart,
About to begin the morning's work.

Catherine Clothier (12)
Homewood School

The Tiger

The tiger crouching in
The long grass ready
To pounce on its
Awaiting prey.

The lightning falls
Like a thousand knives
Spearing through the
Swamp-like sky.

The old willow tree
Lurched in the ruthless
Wind ready to shed
Its golden bullets.

James Cornish (12)
Homewood School

Balloons Up High

Feet flip-flop on the frosty grass,
Rustling feathers all warm and snug,
Squawking pelicans drown the sound of balloons,
Watching the fish like hawks,
Pelicans getting ready for the day ahead.

The ripples on the moat which surrounds,
The beautiful stone castle is bleak and bitter,
The dark grey stone walls protect the warm Heaven inside,
Reflections bring the muddy moat to life.

Roaring into the atmosphere,
All different colours light up the musky sunrise,
The whoosh of heat declares the start of the day,
The balloons start their graceful ascent into the misty sky.

Jessica Cooper (12)
Homewood School

Paradise

The tranquil water trickles slow
A liquid like diamonds glow
And falls onto the wet, velvet rocks below
A silver rush of calm and free water flows

The fresh, uplifting smell is pure and clear
Inviting a luscious evergreen carpet that is almost sheer
Long, pointy evergreen leaves rustle near

Old ancient trees rustle in the chilling breeze
Smothered in a cover of shiny leaves
Eager to please.

Stephanie Chibnall (12)
Homewood School

The Castle

The golden glow of the sun
beams down on the sparkling moat
that surrounds the old majestic castle,
that stands proud like a soldier
coming out of battle victorious.

The pelicans are squawking from the bank
and the flame of the bright blue balloon
roars loudly as it takes off.

The balloon floats slowly upwards
leaving the castle behind to join
the many balloons that are like a swarm
of bees on the pale blue sky.

Frankie Crane (12)
Homewood School

The Countryside

Across the field to the farm,
Where the animals sound like a marching band,
The river flowing back and forth,
And in the distance you hear the neighing horse.

In the trees packed so closely together,
You hear the birds sing their morning song,
The fish in the river are dancing together,
And the croaking frogs are sitting on logs,
The soft, velvet hills which are next to a forest,
Have birds pecking at the apple trees,
The fields behind have haystacks ready for winter.

Anna Bagulay (12)
Homewood School

The Castle Is Watching

The pelican's silky feathers ruffle gently in the wind,
His orange beak glinting as he glides elegantly upwards,
Towards the balloons,
Floating like spectrum bubbles,
Blown by a tiny child.

As the balloons soar onwards,
Silent as the stars,
The castle watches listlessly,
Its dark windows betray no feelings,
As ghostly screams echo along its halls,
Telling tales of old.

And all the while the pelicans,
Grooming their pearly-white coats,
Watchfully gaze as the balloons,
Disappear into the clouds,
And the sky becomes lifeless again.

Becky Bell (12)
Homewood School

The Morning Break

The unspoilt landscape
                        Rolls down the overgrown path
Birds singing in the new day's dawn

                The lake's secrets lay undiscovered
Trees stand tall, whispering their story
          New waves break like prancing white horses

At midday, snakes bask on forgotten faces
    Wind bustles past on its never-ending journey
Shadows run across looking for a place to rest.

Fergus Campbell (12)
Homewood School

The Beach

The sand on the beach is a murky beige,
like that of a wilted leaf falling to the ground
after its reign in autumn.

The trees are so far away and small,
you feel as if the slightest touch from your little finger
would crush them to cinders.

The hotel stands tall and proud,
protective over its people.
Standing proudly,
looking over the waves
as the ongoing crowd
dawdles past without a
care in the world.

Hannah Davis (12)
Homewood School

A Piece Of Mother Nature

The bright hills put the town in darkness
like a shadow from a giant.

The windmill groans as it has to go round and round
pulling all the pine needles off the tree.

The river runs through the town in a race to the sea
leaving its silky trail on the banks.

And we just sit
and watch.

Robert Crawford (12)
Homewood School

Balloon Show

See a colourful balloon show
See cotton wool clouds
See staring pelicans
See an empty crowd

Some balloons high
Some balloons low
All balloons rising
At a hot air balloon show

The castle sits there
Calm and still
By a moat
Near a hill

Pelicans sit there
Calm and steady
Going to fly
Getting ready.

Gavin Curtin (12)
Homewood School

Paradise

The blue, ice crystal pool,
Shimmers and shines like a sparkly ball,
Under the sun's wall.

The vast landscape is really rare,
Like a dotted island with polar bears,
And it is all so bare.

The sky is a beautiful clear blue,
Like a blue shadow coming up to you,
It is almost like it's giving you a clue.

Samantha Batt (12)
Homewood School

Full Moon

The moon shines bright up in the sky,
the trees stand silent nearby.
As the moon starts to disappear,
the sky gets lighter as the meadow draws near.

The wind is whistling in the trees,
the birds are singing in the breeze.
The grass stirs slowly, what can be found?
Only the crickets making a croaking sound.

As the sun rises behind the mountains,
the moon disappears like a waterless fountain.
The pretty colours as the sun sets,
the trees are yawning, it's time to rest.

Billy Beaney (12)
Homewood School

The Morning Forgotten

The morning has been forgotten
The clouds look like cotton
The birds are crying
And the river is slowly dying

The trees are swaying
The animals are praying
And the shiny sun sparkles in the sky

The mountains are so high
The hay is drying
And a road is leading to the sunlight.

Jenna Bertram (12)
Homewood School

The Sunset Ruins

The birds sang in the bright sunset sky,
as the tall trees danced in the slight breeze.
The river sparkled as the bright sun shone down,
the ancient ruins stood quiet and still,
next to a pretty yellow daffodil.

The pathway leading to a view of joy,
the hills looked like a row of pyramids.
As the sunset got brighter, shadows covered the ruins,
and the singing, graceful birds went back to their nests
in the tall, green pine trees.

All went quiet, not a sound, the clouds came along
and covered the bright sunset.
The river stopped shining, the trees stopped dancing
in the slight breeze.
Everything went dead quiet.

Jessica Grimes (13)
Homewood School

The Night Sky Moon

The moon shone bright in the middle of the velvet night.
Fruit covered the trees and the blowing grass.
It was a beautiful sight.

The night sky coloured the mountains and hills a blue velvet.
A sight that I would never forget.

I stood still and looked around.
The trees gently moving in the night-time wind.
Blowing was the only sound.

Jodie Blake (12)
Homewood School

The Stormy Night

Lashing down, the hard, fierce rain.
The tiger racing through the long green grass.
The big beautiful cat, vain.
He needs shelter and food to last.
His furry paws trample the muddy ground.
Gracefully he leaps over a fallen log.
Ears up, he hears a sound.
Suddenly his cold, wet nose smells a big fat hog.

As the furry tiger races through the forest for its prey,
Its starving tummy is rumbling for some food.
The poor fat hog isn't having much of a good day.
The stormy tiger is in a good mood,
Now it's got its food.

The tired tiger, trying to find a place to sleep.
And the poor hog's mum and dad
Weeping for him to come home.

Charlotte Griffiths (12)
Homewood School

The Countryside

The golf fairway is as smooth as a piece of glass.
The path gets deeper into the background.
The sun shines its yellow reflection into the cobalt river.

The flags flutter while the wind is blowing.
The horse clip-clops along the heart of the bridge.
The cockerel wakes you in the morning from your rest.

The crops stretch out when the morning rises.
The windmill propels a strong breeze.
The farm's hay falls out the top of the barn when an animal wakes up.

Terry Bourne (12)
Homewood School

Ever And Ever

Birds flying high above
The fresh blue mountains
Without a care in the world
With no limits
Like a free spirit
Soaring through the open sky.

An old building just lying there
With no hopes
With no dreams
Without a soul
Just lying there.

The water so still
So delicate and peaceful
So much life within
Just keeps on going
For ever and ever.

Leanne Dolman (12)
Homewood School

The Rock

The rock's strength and authority
Overpowers all that stands in the grasp
Of its jagged stone arms.

It stands proud against the light blue sky
Like a high and mighty general overseeing
The well-deserved victory of his tired troops.

The freezing ice lays flat against the majestic rock
Who is wise and powerful
Like a sleeping wizard
Dormant but still alert.

Chris Bottrill (12)
Homewood School

The Harbour Morning

Feel the sharp, jagged cliffs,
like a tiger's jaws.
Birds nestle in the moss and fern
above the spraying waves,
and wait for the fish to arrive.

The bobbing white fishing boats,
are ice cubes floating in a cocktail.
The birds pester the fishermen,
as they heave up their catch,
with their squabbling, squawking racket.

The air tastes salty,
like a plate of steaming chips.
The constant chatter of seabirds,
along with the roaring of the tide,
breaks the silence of the quiet harbour morning.

Stephanie Adams (12)
Homewood School

Landscape

The beautiful light blue sky,
stretching for miles and miles,
was birdless, cloudless and boundless.

A lonely island stood majestically,
on the deep blue sea,
while the extinct volcano lay still.

A quiet but busy town lay,
the sun shining, birds chirping,
whilst the waves hit the sandy shore.

Alice Doucy (12)
Homewood School

The Two Beasts

Through the undergrowth he prowls
On an evening hunt for prey
Then shower turns to downpour - he growls
He knows he must get away

He is an orange blaze against green
His powerful movements trigger fear
A misty haze is all to be seen
He hopes his home is near

Caught out on a wild night
He knows he is in danger
Now there is a crack of light
His whole world looks stranger

He knows he is prey of the storm
By chance he finds a cave
He will stay there until dawn
Now he knows he is saved.

Robert Antrum (12)
Homewood School

Cats

Cats like chasing birds and mice,
cats are fluffy, sweet and nice.
They like sitting in the sun,
and licking butter from a bun.

Cats like hiding in a box,
but don't like hiding with a fox.
Cats like pouncing in the air,
which fluffs up their long, sleek hair.

Cats like running round and round,
cats like sleeping safe and sound.
Cats like playing all day long,
and singing their little cat-like song.

Blue Jenkins (11)
Homewood School

Reflections

Hot air balloons filling the sky
with bursting bright colours
against the lovely blue sky
making beautiful reflection in the water.

The pelicans are sitting as still as statues
waiting for their prey patiently
they start to pounce on their prey
and fly away.

The castle is old and still standing
not moving an inch
the moat is big and peaceful
surrounding the big and powerful fort.

Vickie Fuller (12)
Homewood School

Lightning

The noise of the tiger's feet stomping
on the sharp, crunching twigs underfoot
the trees dancing in the fierce storm
the lightning striking the trees and bringing them down
in the blink of an eye

The sound of the trees creaking
as the wind tries to take them down
and win the fight

The lightning bolt lighting up the dark, murky sky
glistening in the sharp tiger's eyes
thinking God can't fight this evil storm.

Adam Giles (12)
Homewood School

By The Farm

The peacefully quiet village awakens to the morning,
chickens flapping about in the barn.
The clear, cloudless sky washes over the green hills.
Earth is newly ploughed and the plants sprout up like miniature trees.

Cows and sheep come out to feed on the newly rolled-up hay,
as golden as the sun.
A farmer comes to the fields to sow his seeds and
place his scarecrows to frighten the hungry birds.

Village children sing joyfully as they walk to the schoolhouse
across the winding bridge.
A beautiful smell of cookies greeting the school children
as they enter the classroom.
A blazing sun creeps through the classroom blinds
and rests upon the board.

Samantha Gibbons (12)
Homewood School

The Countryside

The sun rises in the old, quiet country,
Nothing but water trickling down the running stream,
Horses' hooves clip-clop at slow pace on the surface of the road,
The black smoke rises, birds choking in the thick air,
        their sight blackened out.

The trees sway in the open wind, leaves fall like water off a cliff face,
The farmer drives in his pitchfork into woven hay,
Cows call out to their fellow friends, the sun goes down to signal
        it's the end of the day.
The light sheds its glow over the dark countryside,
People start packing away and resting for the next day,
The water still running below the bridge, the light reflecting off it,
Nearly blinding people passing by.

William Alkin (12)
Homewood School

The Tropical Storm

In the tropical forest there's a terrible storm,
the trees are fighting furiously with each other.
The rain is crashing onto the leaves,
the grass is like your hair getting drenched as it
touches your legs, trying to stick.

The tiger is running as fast as he can,
trying to find a safe place to stay.
He's scared of the noise the thunder's thumping.
He spots some food, it looks like a deer,
he starts to creep up with his soft, furry paws.
The deer stands up and looks around,
just then the tiger pounces and the deer falls to the floor.

Finally the lightning was striking to the floor,
the tiger had found a safe place to stay.
The thunder was still thumping,
the lightning was lighting up the sky,
and the rain just made the whole thing look dull.

Rebecca Greenfield (12)
Homewood School

Grant Wood

The fresh trees swaying in the fresh air
and the river splashes from side to side.
The seeds popping up with a spike and a furry top.

The lovely fresh grass grows smooth on the hills.
The big bumps in the distance look so bright,
they glow in the light of the sun.

The trees stretch right up to the sun to grow.
The grass smells like it has just been cut.

Jade Farrin (12)
Homewood School

Pelicans And Balloons

Soaring high,
brightly coloured bags of gas
move over the castle walls.
Shapes swishing swiftly
over the moat like fast cars.

Black and white pelicans with orange beaks
getting ready to have a dip
and have a little lick and some fun.
The golden glow on the castle
shining in their eyes.

The fluffy trees dance in the breeze
the big, dark castle
standing proud around
the fast flowing water.

Matthew Hogg (12)
Homewood School

Lurking In The Shadows

A tiger lurks in the plants,
Out of view, baring its white, sharp teeth,
Heart beating, silent breaths.

All around a fierce storm,
Flashing and crashing, scoring through the sky,
Rain pelting down.

Plants and trees crashing,
Like gallant monsters,
Lurking over his head, whistling in the wind.

Elouise Ellis (12)
Homewood School

The Looking Full Moon

The bright moonlight shining onto the roof of the tree.
Some leaves in the tree were dancing.
Fields behind were playing a game of hedges.
Soft moon was happily watching everyone having fun.

Glittering green leaves on the roofs of the trees.
Some fields on the horizon look like a fluffy, lumpy, patchwork quilt.

The berries on the trees look like bee stings.

Joshua Earland (12)
Homewood School

Sabre-Tooth World

The mountain line reaches up to the clear sky,
Trees, bushes and shrubs cover these giants like a thick layer of fur.

A herd of macrauchenia have a midday drink.
The shallow lake is a brilliant blue, fresh water stream,
That runs right through the territory of a pack of smilodon.

The pack of two-fanged terrors,
Look on at the herd of macrauchenia gently drinking,
Unaware that one will be picked as prey.

Aiden Gorham (12)
Homewood School

The Tiger

See the tiger wandering in the rainforest looking very vicious
Smiling, looking like a hunter shooting for his dinner.

Hear the storm starting and the tigers roaring
And running to their shelters.

Feel the cold air drifting on your face
And the grass drifting into your hands.

Russell Dullaway (12)
Homewood School

The Tiger

The thunder plays as a drum
The black, cloudy sky is cracked in half
By the lightning shooting
Across the sky.

The trees whistled and the
Green glowing plants staring at
The tiger and its razor-sharp teeth
As it awaits its prey.

As the rain shoots down
On the waving leaves and plants
The tiger pounds
Through the grass.

Danielle Groat (12)
Homewood School

The Li Jiang

The clear waters of the Li Jiang,
Flow between sheer rounded hills,
Like a robin flying gracefully,
Through the still air.

Trees scattered along the edge,
Of the rough, sandy earth,
Like a flock of sheep,
Walking through a field.

The canoe floating peacefully,
Upon the still, reflecting water,
As quiet and lonely,
As a fox lost on a mountainside.

Jaime Golding (12)
Homewood School

The Sunset Chase

As red as blood the sunset,
Like ice his tears froze over the river,
It seemed to him as a sacrifice,
He was being watched with evil eyes,
There was nothing he could do,
He was being chased like a pack of hounds after a fox,
There was no escape.

A midnight party boat,
Came sailing down the river,
The bridge was like a fairground,
Shining into the sky at night,
In between two paradise islands,
The tall palm trees swished from side to side.

The reflections of the lights shot across the river like
Pastels smudged across a painting,
The vibrant smudges streamed across the whole river,
Only leaving black from the paradise islands.

Amy Guess (13)
Homewood School

The Balloon Race

The clouds look like familiar faces,
As the balloons float peacefully
In the bright blue sky.
The brown, brick castle shines in the light,
The balloons and the castle
Are reflected in the rippled moat.
On the lush green grass
Are the confused pelicans,
Who can see their reflection,
Not the fish.

Joshua Dunk (12)
Homewood School

Lonely Castle

The castle stands rotting away through history
Its only enemy now is time.
The tattered walls crumbling and destroyed
After its many wars.

Outside, golden dandelions basking in the sun
The garden awash with many colours.
They stand wavering in the wind
Like people doing the Mexican wave.

Above them the clouds hover
Floating in the calm breeze.
They bounce along the sky
Like sheep in a meadow.

It is all green in the garden and full of wildlife
Shadowed in the castle's glory.

Ben Hawkes (12)
Homewood School

Tenerife

The warm sea air captures people from miles around
The sunbathers are not restless as they cannot hear a sound

The sand is hot and the temperature's at its peak
The beach is so enchanting you could stay there for a week

The parasols keep you shady and as healthy as can be
You're glad you're out of school but you sure don't miss the sea

The sky is blue, the air is hot, the sea's as clear as glass
The flowers rob the beach and the sand's as bright as brass

The sunny, sandy, sunlit beach will open its gaping doors
I cannot think what else to write so I'll end this with a pause.

Nabil Graham (12)
Homewood School

The Badminton Game

The shuttlecock swishing through the air
The wind whistling through the girl's hair
Trees towering tall above
The girls giggling, such sisterly love.

The bright blue sky, still and calm
The grass glistening in the shining summer sun
The house proudly stands
Gazing and watching closely.

The colours are beautiful
Blues and greens
It looks so stunning
The best I've seen.

Amy Hilding (12)
Homewood School

The Lonely Bed And Breakfast

In the old street, the bed and breakfast stood
with his mouth wide open
gazing at the crowds of men fighting in the street
the crunch of a man's nose made the crowd howl
as blood dripped down his face.

The crowd was howling once more
as he tried to pull the man down
they pushed and pulled as the cold breeze blew down the street.

He had been a manager of a big posh hotel
but his dreams had been shattered when people started fighting
all he could do was stand and gaze at the crowd around him.

Sophie Hilden (12)
Homewood School

Exmoor On My Mind

There's a line when water meets the shore,
Blue sea touching silty sand as black as coal,
Overlooked by lazy pot-bellied rolling hills,
So many shades of copper and green,
One hand alone has not the fingers to count them.

Like a king upon his castle,
I stand atop the Tor,
As witness to nature's magnificence,
A kingdom of rugged harmony.

Bright blue bay beyond black beach,
Distant horizon in my palm but out of reach,
Tranquillity interrupted by the hiss of the breeze,

That I must follow when I leave.

Rhys Maynard (12)
Homewood School

Girly

Being girly is *sooo* not easy,
you can't cough, burp or be sneezy.
When you buy something you have to think,
will it go with anything pink?
We must look good,
and so we should.
We've got boxes of make-up,
next to the cutsie pup,
and our piles of bags,
one for every time the dog wags.
They say that diamonds are a girl's best friend,
but truthfully, the list never ends!

Sophie Goldstein (12)
Homewood School

Oslo

The Norwegian flag flies high,
Into the frosty midday sky,
The slender branches and the trees' smooth barks,
Edge the avenue of the snow-clad park.
The people scurry from their closely parked cars,
To the warmth of the welcoming bars.
Days are short at this time of year,
But people still linger over their frosty beers.
Christmas is coming so they shouldn't delay,
So they should soon drink up and be on their way.
Shops will be busy, frantic and loud,
So hurry, drink up, so we miss the crowd,
I'm glad that's over, let's be on our way,
I'm really exhausted with such a frantic day.

Martyn Luck (12)
Homewood School

The Seashore

The beautiful sphere is standing serenely
shining intensively alongside the sky,
it is the sun gleaming its daylight shine,
like a lightbulb in disguise.

The water is a crystal clear colour
stacking up its boats on its harbour shelves,
while the matured horses are pulled
by the weary workers themselves.

In the background of the inspiring landscape painting,
the fishermen's stone cottages
stand opposite the sand
on the fishermen's boats and nets.

David Lincoln (13)
Homewood School

Mountains In The Mist

Silent mountains shrouded in silver,
Hold their secrets with majestic power,
What have they experienced in times past?
What will they witness when this life is a memory?

The gentle waters of Lake Llanberis,
Twinkling like dewdrops in the evening sun, what mysteries
                              does it lock away?
Waters grace the soft shoreline like folds of velvet,
Leaving the rustling reeds standing proud, like soldiers.

The whistling wind sweeps carpets of lush, green grass,
Northwards and southwards,
Protecting all animals and birds,
Playful children run like the deer,
Prancing, hopping, skipping.

Lizzie Phipps (12)
Homewood School

Nobody Knew

The treacherous mountains, misty blue, lie above the lake,
Enveloped in mist that is rising upward,
Isolating them from everything,
What lay behind them? Nobody knew.

Sitting in the lake is a lonely island,
Dense woodland clothes it,
Was it inhabited? Nobody knew.

Nestled amongst the trees are buildings of great quality,
They stand majestically on the mountainside,
How long until developers come? Nobody knew.

Harry Higginson (12)
Homewood School

Blue Skies

The blue sky covers everything like a big blanket
With a few wispy clouds in it
And a small moon strangely out in the day
Smiling at the people below.

Below, people play badminton
Screeching as they hit the shuttle.
Up into the sky towers a big bush
With the fragrance of a Christmas tree.

A big, posh-looking house stands majestically.
The rough texture of the bricks stand out from
                          the ivy crawling up the wall.
A mower can be heard two gardens away, chugging along.
The smell of freshly-cut grass wafts into the open windows.

Daniel Oliver (12)
Homewood School

No-Man's-Land

The bright shine of the full moon
onto the colourful fields and the tall bushes,
which shades the trunks,
the moon makes the sky different shades of blue
like it's relaxing.

The rough fields in the horizon make it look like a patchwork blanket.
The tree looks like it's dancing around in the half light shine.

The moon's sad glowing makes the fields feel lonely and dull
when they could be all happy, jumping around
instead of staying still like no-man's-land.

Eleanor Hayward (12)
Homewood School

Beauty Of Nature

In the far distance stands a towering mountain,
Covered in snow it withstands the ice-cold.
Raging winds pelt the structural giant.

In the mid-ground lies a mirror of nature,
It is a home to many creatures of the deep.
Surrounding trees are also homes for scurrying squirrels.

In the foreground is a dazzling array of colour.
Majestic pinks and blues cover the world in a carpet of beauty.

Matthew Mansfield (12)
Homewood School

The Dark Night

The big, stripy, smelly tiger prowling through the jungle
with razor-sharp teeth ready to break you and your bones in half.

The big, green, spiky, sharp jungle
with leaves holding on for dear life against the biting storm.

The noise of the breaking twigs like bones shattering
while the trees were bouncing from side to side
whilst overhead lightning crackles the dark night sky.

Billy Hands (12)
Homewood School

Brandeglio

The towering mountains topped with snow
like iced cakes in a bakery.
The church sits in the centre of the village
surrounded but sticks out like a sore thumb.
Children play in the streets
making the most of the snow before it melts.

Michael Rice (12)
Homewood School

Silver Eye Over Silbury Hill

The full moon shines brightly over the rich green fields
like the sky's silver eye scanning the land for any problems.
It spreads its light over the hills like butter over bread.
Everything is frozen, stopped dead.

The rolling hills run in the background covered with fields and trees
like a blanket covering the cold earth.
The land is lonely and left.

A jungle covered my sight as I got closer.
There were bushy trees with damp,
wild, rotten-smelling berries dotted around on them.
I knew that to get to the city I would have to
crunch through the busy, berry, brushy trees.
When I left I also knew that Silbury Hill would be waiting for the morning
and yet another lonely traveller over the wonderful Silbury Hill.

Megan Lee (12)
Homewood School

Paradise In Barbados

As the waves hit the rocks, lightly and slow,
the soft sand rippled with the water,
and in-between the big, hard rocks,
a little baby crab scurried across the shore.

The little, quiet house beside the harbour,
received a cool, calming breeze.
High up from the jagged rocks,
the tall, high palm trees swung and swayed.

A long way out where the sea is deep,
the waves grew stronger and the fish got bigger.
Up above in the great blue sky,
not a cloud was in sight, just clear blue.

Michael Laity (13)
Homewood School

A Cry Of Mercy

As I strolled through a roaring crowd of bravery,
I never knew what lay before me.

I found myself marching into many distraught lives.
Drawing nearer to a crowd who begged for mercy,
and ran in circles of pandemonium.

I started to feel a sharp pain of regret.
I marched on until I needed to stop from my regret.

Then the troops were led into a hole
full of slush and soldiers' boredom.

As we were led into blooming slush,
it grew into a flood of poppies
from blazing fire of helpless bodies.

Crashing into a mouldy stench,
soldiers screamed and shouted, 'Gas, gas, quick run.'

I saw a young boy wounded from a shot.
He begged for mercy as he suffocated
in a green cloud of smoke.

My pain of regret got worse.
It was turning to guilt as well.

All I thought of was the young boy
drowning in a green cloud of gas.

My pain has sharpened, I couldn't see.
All I saw was a red blur in my hands.

I heard the soldiers counting,
'I, 2, 3, and the dead and wounded thrown
onto a cart to be taken away from the battle.'

And what I heard was me.

Michelle King (11)
Homewood School

Mountain Country Poem

Amongst the hills lay tiny cottages.
In the field people play with a sparkling,
red, shiny ball that glistens in the baby, blue sky.
They play like animals in a hot jungle.
Jolly people are chuckling as they play
amongst the piles of rustling, playful leaves.
Inside the cottage the bricks dance to the
beating music as a noisy party takes place.

The breeze sails through people's ears like a
small sailing boat going to Dunkirk to collect
wounded soldiers from the victimising cruel war.
The gentle whisper of talking, excited leaves
whip through the air as the branches on the big,
bold, bright trees snap with happiness.
The water trickles through the opening gap in the hills.

Climbers battle their way through the fierce, friendly, ferocious trees.
The smell of dirt from ploughed fields spin
and bang against the laughing trees.
The grass along the barking, brown, big trees,
bark tickles the trees like Mr Tickle from the Mr Men books.
As the water trickles through the hills,
the sun beats down, warming, tanning people and Earth.

Gabrielle McNamara (12)
Homewood School

The Building

Without a cloud in the colossal clear blue sky,
The sun stands tall and bright,
The walls of the building are long and overblown.
They are as white as snow and as rough as a sheet of sandpaper.
The dark green doors stands still and thin
Against the white wall like a grizzly bear in the North Pole.

Tom Wood (12)
Homewood School

Paradise

The horses graze
Among the grass
The hours of the day
Quickly pass

There are flowers growing
On the grassy verge
The colours of the scene
In the river merge

The riverbed
Is stoned and cobbled
And in the wind
The trees wobbled

A group of birds
Flock in the sky
With elegant wings
South they fly.

Jade Pearman (12)
Homewood School

Bird Boat Lake

The dew sparkles like diamonds
on the ruins of the ancient villa

Tiny black specks of ink
in the pastel colours of the sky

Children rowing to the island of reeds,
laughter echoes from long ago.

Kirsty Parsons (12)
Homewood School

The Watcher

Nothing is as foul as fear itself
I have learnt this well
For people never listen
To a word I tell

I should know
What to expect
I've been there
Got the T-shirt

Don't shoot the messenger
He only brings the message
Same as the priest
Who can only bless it

For I am the watcher
You cannot hide
I see your face
The pain is inside

For I am the watcher
Escape if you can
There's no hope
I see the life of man.

Rachel White (14)
Homewood School

The Seaside

Inside the trees the only shade is flooded
with people whilst the sun beams down.

The caves fill with water and fish and crabs
get stranded as the tide goes out.

The sun fades away across the sea
and all the land to reveal only darkness.

Amy Neil (12)
Homewood School

Luminous Sky

Fluffy cotton wool swoops through the bright sky,
The clouds leap like baby lambs,
Ducking and diving through the dense trees,
Until night falls and brings the chase to an end.

The misshapen moon sparkles in the ever-darkening sky,
Hiding its fading face amongst the floating lace,
Piercing the luminous sky with its radiant sheen,
Wishing itself to disappear into darkness.

Towering trees shadow over the vibrant grass,
Looming high above the precise mansion,
Leaning towards where the sparkling sun should be,
Hoping it shall soon appear to make the picture complete.

Charlotte Wyatt (13)
Homewood School

Sunlit Solitude

A sinister hole appears in the sky,
Through this breach the sun's rays are swallowed,
Beaming down on sunbathers who lie.

The strong, white clouds crowd the sky,
Their commanding presence, majestically they cry,
'We will surround the plane as it does fly.'

The colossal plane forsakenly flies through the sky,
Like the Titanic left alone to die,
An English flag on the back wing shows its loyalty,
For England it will sing.

David Neill (12)
Homewood School

The Volcanoes

The cold, white sky is providing
curtains behind the towering volcanoes,
while the flaming sun beats down,
toasting the burnt land.

The sharp green fir trees,
covering the volcanoes like a carpet,
while near the very top there is
nothing but rough rock.

The uneven pathway through the steep volcanoes
bends and curves -
cars spraying mud and rocks on their tail,
until you get to the crater
where the view is spectacular.

Fleur Schrapel (12)
Homewood School

Scandinavian Dream

The tranquil silence passes over the mountains.
The vast openness of the wildlife towers over the lake.
The hilly mountains overlook the skyline.

The cloudy sky spreads across the horizon.
Snowy mountain tops reach into the sky.
Masses of flowers drift into the lake.

The forest conceals the hidden villages.
Little islands float around in the aquamarine lake.
The azure sky expands for miles around.

Alice Murton (12)
Homewood School

Jungle Tiger

Jungle tiger eyeing its prey
Jungle tiger has to slay
Waiting for its guard to drop
Through the jungle he never stops.

Hunting in the rattling rain
From his last fight he's in terrible pain,
Jungle tiger is soaking wet,
It's been a week since he last ate.

The bushes open like doors as he walks through,
His prey doesn't even have a clue,
Then bang, out he leaps like a horse out of its gate,
An hour later his prey is in a terrible state.

Adrian Worsley (12)
Homewood School

Twilight Café

In a town your eyes will look at the textured, purple sky,
A horse and carriage trots down the street as the stars
                              twinkle and sparkle,
And the sight makes a house at the back look like a silhouette.

To the main source of the art, which includes the bright café,
And whilst the customers are busy chatting and eating,
A dark shadow hides behind the doorway.

Down to the detailed trees as they make the wind whistle,
It makes a nice naturalistic sound as it rustles the leaves,
The twilight café makes a nice glow to keep it beautiful.

Dylan Troeger (12)
Homewood School

The Old Crumbly Tomb By A Lake

Far away, above the hills, the birds, they play,
In the pastel sky of yellow, orange, red and grey.
The upside down world reflects on the lake,
And in the corner, the bold tomb, standing bold
Like a lioness protecting her young.

The smooth, silky water glistening like crystals,
So smooth it is like you can see a plane of glass over it,
And when I drop a stone into it,
It is like when you smash the smooth glass and ruin the silence.

The only sounds are the birds tweeting,
Only being broken when the wind has enough strength.
The autumn leaves of red, orange and yellow.

Oliver Sargeant (12)
Homewood School

The Game

Two ladies playing badminton in the morning light,
in the background with morning dew
which shines like big crystals in the clear sunlight.

There is a light breeze in the air,
with the birds singing in the bush and
the light breeze tickling the leaves
with the smell of morning earth in the air.

The trees are standing there
listening to the swoosh of badminton racquets
and the chattering of the two ladies in the morning sunlight.

Ben Squires Quinn (13)
Homewood School

Jungle Fright!

Crouching down in the long jungle grass,
The jungle noises surrounding you with fear,
The lightning and the thunder covering the sky,
Soaring down and thumping the ground,
The rain starts to pour and smacks you in the face,
Like stinging icicles running down your back,
Giving you shivers as it soaks you through.
Above you, trees screaming as they are being pushed
Side to side by the howling wind.
Leaves rattling, while branches are wildly swaying in the storm.

Just in front of you, you can smell danger up ahead,
Then you see something, something that is moving in the long grass,
You get a glimpse of an orange and black-stripped creature.
Its head pokes up and back down through the grass,
As quick as a bullet and then it starts crawling again,
Then it stops.
Your back's aching by crouching down too long,
Your bare feet hurting on the rough ground,
Your heart, thumping in fright.
The creature crawls near you,
Its teeth as sharp as pieces of broken glass.
Its paws are huge, good for killing things.
It's hard to keep quiet
So it doesn't see you.

Bang!
The lightning hits a tree.
You jump.
The creature looks in your direction.
You're not sure if it's spotted you.
You keep your head down,
The creature then slowly goes down,
Ready to pounce.
Crack!
You look behind you, the tree near you has been hit.
Crack!
The tree slowly tips,
Crash!

The tree hits the ground,
Thankfully not near you.
The tree flat on the floor, dead.
Looking through the branches and leaves,
You spot the creature,
It's okay,
It's crouching cautiously,
Stunned by the incident.
It looks around,
Its ear twitched back,
It checks the all-clear,
And turns around,
It's too scared to pounce on
Whatever it was about to pounce on.
It starts to run frantically and furiously
At not catching its meal.
The creature runs and runs,
Until it disappears,
Into the rainy mist.

Freya Walker (12)
Homewood School

Carriage Driver

As the horse and carriage clip-clop down the cold, bumpy street,
Braving the cold which lashes at them violently,
The man on the back looks around.
He sees people huddling around their warm tea,
Like birds huddled together on a cold winter's day.
Some people rush home to sit in front of a nice warm fire.
As the carriage driver gets closer,
He can hear the chattering of customers' teeth,
And see steam rising out of their mugs,
Like a steam engine on a cold damp dewy morning.

Kiefer Sim (12)
Homewood School

The Rampaging Wind
(Based on van Gogh - Wheat Fields And Cypress Trees)

The clouds swirl around,
In their never-ending way,
The mountains stand tall,
Prodding the crystal blue sky.

The tall trees tremble in the wind,
The dirty rocks clatter together,
As the wind continues to howl like a roaring bear,
Swaying the bushes as it rampages.

The coarse grass sways vigorously,
Bending like a piece of rubber,
The few that don't make it back up,
Lie on the floor,
They will face the wind no more.

Ben Vincer (13)
Homewood School

The Veranda

The sun cast its light over the deep valley
The snow-covered houses looked like cakes
In the window of a fully-stocked bakery

An ice fisher braved the biting cold to catch fish for his family
With just a dog for a friend.

But the veranda was a bomb shelter
From the past raid of snow bombs
Which had covered the surrounding war zone
In its white blanket.

Jonathan White (12)
Homewood School

The Tiger In The Storm

The sky was as black as pitch,
Until lit up by the glowing white string,
As it sewed the seams across the velvet blanket.
The skeleton-like trees rebirthed
As the wild animals danced and sung across the branches,
Bringing music to the trees' ears.
Rain droplets manoeuvred across the jagged-surfaced bark
Of the skeletons.

Tickly leaves waved as the smaller ground animals
Escaped the grass monster.
Walking bushes swished through the stalks of grass.
The sea of green danced to the collisions of thunder.
Dense emerald green blinded your eyes as it surrounded you
With its army.
Hissing sticks glided along the earth like eels through water.

A streak of orange fire laid in the grass.
Its black stripes making him invisible amongst the long stalks.
A growl or purr of friendliness it may seem,
As he smiled at his innocent prey.

He pounced . . .

Crunch!

His claws sunk into the furry creature.
Desperate screams of the citizens of the jungle
Flew into the stormy sky.
Scarlet-red clashed with the emerald green
As fresh flesh was ripped from the body mercilessly.
He grinned again and grabbed the body,
And pulled it into the dense forest.
Where he could eat his midnight meal in peace!

Hollie Weatherill (12)
Homewood School

The Motionless Castle

The motionless castle,
Trapped and silent for hundreds of years,
The castle as rough as the road,
The moat as smooth as the tabletop.

The grass smells sweet,
It's like a mini jungle,
For the ants to march about,
In search of food for a feast.

Hot air balloons pulling their
Cords to lift into
The cotton wool-like clouds,
And birds singing as if they're in an opera.

There lies the castle watching,
As infant birds take flight,
The hot air balloons fly into the daylight,
But the castle lies still and quiet.

Daniel Warren (12)
Homewood School

My Cool Pets

He's small and cool for he lives in water.
He makes a noise all night.
He has a mate called Poo,
Who likes to do kung fu.

You'll never guess what we are.
We like to get around
But not in a car.

We replaced two others
Who came to a sticky ending.
That Thomas is cool
Especially when he plays the guitar.

Yes we are the answer to his wish
Please God give me two goldfish.

Tom Eaton (11)
Mascalls School

Her

I feel like dirt
Whenever she looks at me
I'm really hurt
I'd rather die than be near her

She's surrounded by boys
While I stand alone
Them all giving her priceless toys
As I long for only someone

I see her daddy pick her up in his flash car
While I walk scuffing my shoes
As she's sitting in her home bar
I'm nursing my baby brother

When we have the test
She gets top marks
She's the best
While I'm the dirt.

Victoria Mayrick (11)
Mascalls School

Friends

Friends are people you hang around with,
Share secrets with.

Friends are people who are always there for you,
To care for you.

Friends are people who care for you,
Always there for you.

Friends are people who laugh with you,
Talk with you.

Friends are people who you talk out problems with,
Share a shoulder with.

Friends are people you fall out with,
Then make up with.

Christina Bridger (12)
Mascalls School

Mr Tomato

How does it feel to have no nose?
Does it feel as bad as having no toes?
You having nothing to wriggle when the weather gets cold
And nothing to blow when you go down with a cold.
When you feel upset what do you do?
When you are excited do you roll over with happiness?
Oh, Mr Tomato what do you do?

Why is your hair such a bright, bright green?
What would be your one wish if you could have anything?
Would you like to meet the Queen?
Would you fly,
Or would you prefer arms and legs?
What would you wish for Mr Tomato?

If you were a person what would you wear?
Would you have long or short hair?
Would your voice be deep or high?
What would be your favourite colour?
Would you ride a bike?
Where would you live?
Mr Tomato what would you do?

I wonder if you'd like me?

Billie Pingault (11)
Mascalls School

Autumn

Cold and wet, windy and bright
the fire is burning throughout the night.
Coal is roaring, ashes are singeing
time for bed, children are whinging.

Leaves are falling to the ground
the wind is blowing all around.
Birds are flying with no sound
the hops are falling to the ground.

Katie Davison (12)
Mascalls School

Autumn

The rubbish is as smelly as a dustbin,
The cars roar past like a train,
The trees flutter in the breeze like a bird flying
The sheep are nowhere to be seen.

The birds hop around like a kangaroo
The seagulls are flying like a kite on a very windy day,
The butterflies are gone now,
The trees have gone pale,
Like a very, very gloomy, gloomy day.

The sky is white,
White like snow,
The sun has gone,
Like a day with lots of woe,
The trees are moulting
Like a duck with no feathers.

Rebekka Chamberlain (12)
Mascalls School

Fighting For Freedom

She was a tiger, a vicious animal.
She was vicious because she was caught and put in the zoo.
Lonely, frightened and frustrated,
Once she had lived in the jungle
With her mum, dad, sister and brother.
Now she's in the zoo, trapped and scared.
She gets fed very little in the zoo.
In the jungle she used to have lots of meat.
They were the old times, she had to think of the future.
She got scared when people looked in her cage,
She growled at them and they pointed and stared even more!
I wish I was in the jungle with my mum, dad, sister and brother!

Jasmin Allen (11)
Mascalls School

Think Of . . .

Think of the war with the people who died,
Think of the soldiers who put aside their pride
Think of the trenches
And all those awful stenches
Think of the past, just think.

Think of the Victorians with all their inventions
Think of the children with the work extensions
Think of the past, just think.

Think of the 70s with the Beatles and punks
Think of their fashion with hair like a skunk's
Think of the 70s with laughter and fun
So there's plenty of thinking for everyone.

Amy Prior (11)
Mascalls School

My Holiday To Spain

We went on holiday to Spain,
It was so nice it didn't rain.

The sun was hot,
We burnt a lot.

The pool was cool,
It cooled us down.

We spent some money in the town,
To buy some suncream to make us brown.

The entertainment was quite hot,
Unfortunately the kids' club - not!

Natasha Nichols (11)
Mascalls School

Football Disaster

It was the cup final,
We had won every game,
It was the cup final,
We had driven our fans insane,
But the match today was the most important,
We had to win,
But all our players are as sad as sin,
For the goalie had a bit of a snooze
And then we knew we'd surely lose.
Then in the end we lost 8-0
And we all knew we'd lost our skill.
Back to the drawing board,
Back to our base,
Then the manager slapped my face.

Nick McKee (12)
Mascalls School

Friends

Everyone needs friends, I do,
I would be lost without friends.
Friends are for loving and caring
Not for hating and snaring.
Friends are also for helping and not
For making fun of you.
A friend can't be as sly as a fox,
A friend should be as strong as an ox
For you.

That's what I think about friends.
Think about what I have said
And think to yourself,
Are you a good friend?

Adam El-Bir (12)
Mascalls School

The Phantom Of The Night

The silver moon is rising from the dark depths of the underworld.
All is still, not a sound until the phantom of the night swoops down.
His marble eyes shine in the light of the full moon.
As he hovers throughout the night sky, no mice, rats or voles
Dare to disobey him.
He perches on a branch to rest his tired wings,
His sharp brown eyes scanning every dark corner in case his prey
Tries to hide.
For he is a great seeker.
As he swiftly glides through the air
His dagger-like claws cut the silence.
His long steady wings are decorated
With gold feathers which are organised in such an elegant way.
His cruel, hooked beak,
The killing machine is sparkling in the moonlight,
The cold winter's wind scratching at his feathers,
As he flies high up into the heavens,
The bright sun is rising.
The moon is forced once again to sink deep
Into the depths of the underworld.
He flies home quickly to his nest,
Where he tucks his head under his wings
And begins to dream wonderful thoughts.
Sweet dreams the phantom of the night.

Hayley Sterling (11)
Mascalls School

Monkey

M arvellous tail swinging like branches on a tree
O verwhelming jumping strength
N uts they may eat but they still are strong
K eeping up is very hard, they are just too quick
E lectronic navigation they possess
Y et still they sometimes fail.

George Willock (11)
Mascalls School

The Rhyme Of Innocence

When I hear the slamming of the front entrance next door,
I know she is home from work,
If I wait a few minutes until the clock strikes five,
I'll hear no sound of a dinner fork.

The one I will hear is the one of a child,
A child with a joyous, pleased laugh,
Another present it must be,
Soon it will be time for a bath.

'No, no,' the scream would scream,
'I want to play with my new toy!'
Then there's a sigh, a sigh to say, 'Of course,'
'Thank you,' a voice says, it definitely can't be a boy!

They love that child they really do,
I let out a little laugh,
Then I smile, a smile that says,
The excitement's not finished, not even by half.

Alex Flegg (12)
Mascalls School

Autumn

A ll the leaves are falling to the frostbitten ground,
   the most spectacular colours, reds, yellows, oranges and browns.
U nder ground the foxes, badgers, mice and rabbits
   are getting ready to hibernate all winter long.
T he children are writing their list to
   Santa Claus.
U nder the trees the hedgehogs sleep, beneath piles of
   dead, brown leaves.
M iles of slippery, muddy fields where the rain has fallen
   and the crops have been used.
N oisy birds chirp in the cold and crisp morning.

Laura Gledhill (12)
Mascalls School

9/11

3,600 are trapped, so trapped
They can't get out. The building is collapsing.
The heat, the pain, the horror.
Thunder, like a herd of elephants stampeding
Thumping to nowhere.

7,200 fists beat upon doors, where openings once were
Buckled and twisted. Suffocating black smog.
The waiting, the fear, the numbness.
No one can come. No one can save them
We are all hysterically scarred
The famous Twin Towers standing no more.
Sandstorms laced with smoke snaked around the streets
Is my hand in front of my face? Where is my hand?

People trapped, screaming for help, no one can come.
Why us? Why? As hopes crash to dust.
From this day the world has changed, hopes changed.
Silence.
Memories all trapped forever.

Emily Milton (11)
Mascalls School

The Sky Is As Dull As Reading The Dictionary

The clouds are as fluffy as sheep
The frost on the grass is like 1,000 diamonds
The magpies are black and white, like a sea full of zebras.
The trees are as bushy as a lion's mane
The falling leaves are as bright as a raging warm fire
The hedges are as perfect as a jungle
The wind is as strong as a champion weightlifter
The sunset is as beautiful as a swooping eagle
The sky is as black as a chimney sweep's clothes.

Katherine Whalesby (12)
Mascalls School

Fair Trade

Chocolate, chocolate, it's really nice,
Hopefully it's helping someone's life,
But is it? I wonder, as I look on the shelf,
Cadbury and Nestlé I pick for myself.
Until I see just lying there,
A chocolate bar labelled *Fair,*
'What does it mean?' I asked my mum,
She said, 'I don't know, let's try some.'
It tasted creamy, simply divine,
My brother was jealous and wanted mine.
Fair trade, fair trade, what can it be?
It's obvious really, can you not see?
A bar that helps people who grow the beans,
By giving them more money, that's what it means!

Georgia Hebborn (12)
Mascalls School

The Polar Bear

I'm cold, really cold
The weather is freezing.
But, luckily for me
I've got my lovely warm coat.

But it's not all good.
Sometimes we get hunted down,
By these things
They have huge feet and shout a lot.

With my gnashing jaws and almighty claws
Anything is terrified to come near.
But under all the fur
There really is a kind heart!

Carolyn Bassett (11)
Mascalls School

Sparkling Snowflakes

I am from the clouds of frosty heaven
where secrets are softly woven in silver silk,
I was once a dress of a beautiful snow angel,
My sparkling perfection is created in the
weightless clouds,
I whisper to you from the soft sky before I fall.

I am a frosty feeling of cold heaven,
I gently start my descent,
The clouds command me to carry their
frosty whispers,
Our hearts are on your sleeves when I land,
Then I crash to the ground to start again.

Beverley Williams (12)
Mascalls School

It's Dark . . . It's Time . . .

The wolf stands silent, spying on the sheep,
Ready to pounce and bite.
Waiting near . . . till the coast is clear,
Ready to grab them with its might.

The stars are sparkling in the night,
No clouds to be seen.
The wolf's eyes gleam, its breath is steam,
But the mouth is drooling, mad and mean.

The wolf runs! Like the wind!
Frightening a few birds away.
The sheep gets scared. It wouldn't dare!
But all will be revealed in the day.

Hasna Miah (12)
Mascalls School

Dream

I look out of the window,
A tree whispers in the wind.
The smell of the autumn air
Makes me feel like I can't give in.

I look up at the sky,
The clouds drift so freely.
The sky starts to slowly darken,
The raindrops trickle down the windowpane.

The rain gets heavier,
Starts spiking the ground,
It makes me feel all warm inside.
The day is coming to an end,
The sun is slowly setting.

The night is here,
The stars come out.
The darkness crackles as the moon rises,
I settle down to dream.

Carys Nicholls (12)
Mascalls School

A Wonderful Summer's Day!

On this wonderful summer's day
I see birds high up in the sky
Like small blobs of ink
On a sheet of blue paper.
I see trees as green as a park field
And flowers as bright as a rainbow.

I see the summer sun like a golden penny
Tossed up onto a bright blue sea.
I see a clear blue sky like a settled river
No one around to make a sound but me!

Megan Lumley (12)
Mascalls School

The Witch Of Madoom

Over the mountains dark,
Long river flows with fish in wake,
The gloomy sky coated with clouds,
Forbids all singing for the night,
And in a cave deep and dull,
Sits the Witch of Madoom.

She sits there rigid and quaky,
In her deep, dull cave,
Where bats linger and rats scuttle,
In the deepest, dimmest part of the hole,
Sits the Witch of Madoom.

At the break of dawn,
She walks out into the town,
And all the villagers stop and stare,
At the Witch of Madoom.

'She is so ugly,' they say and exclaim,
But as she nears them they stop and look scared,
For she turns people into bats and rats they declare,
As the Witch of Madoom grows near.

'But she's so sad I don't think she's that bad,'
Exclaimed Rick the blacksmith,
But everyone just laughed,
'You must be mad,' they scowled at him,
As the Witch of Madoom went past.

She went to the graveyard and sat down at a grave,
Nobody knew whose grave it was,
She visited each day,
It was the shape of a cross and covered in moss,
The grave where the Witch of Madoom was sat.

She wished with all her might,
She yelled into the night,
'I want to be a normal human again!'
And from the night she got a fright,
A voice was calling, 'The Witch of Madoom.'

She followed the voice,
It lead her through Madoom
And to a moss-covered grave,
The voice told the Witch of Madoom,
'If you can do one good turn for someone
You can live and die as a human again,
Witch of Madoom.'

She then set out looking for someone in need
And the first person she found was Rick,
She asked, 'What's wrong?'
And to her surprise he didn't run away,
He just looked at her and said,
'I'm lonely, I wish I had a friend,'
To the Witch of Madoom.

She looked at him and smiled,
I know what I can do, she thought,
I shall be his best friend
And be with him always,
Thought the Witch of Madoom.

She asked him to be her friend
And he accepted gratefully
And her good deed was done,
She was covered in green smoke
And the next thing she knew,
She was a lovely young lady,
So she was no longer the Witch of Madoom.

Susie Collings (13)
Mascalls School

Autumn

The sky was as white as a wedding dress.
The leaves on the tree were like green drops of paint.
The grass was as green as a freshly picked bean.
The seagulls were as white as a dove in the sky.
The hills were like moulds of green.
The birds in the sky were like swiftly flying jets.

Nathalie Hill (13)
Mascalls School

The Nothing

The destitute beggar sits on his corner
of the forbidden streets.
As he sits there thousands of people pass
the *nothing* with not a care but only a look.
In his eyes you see sorrow as they fill with a tear
of disrespect and filth.

The destitute beggar sits on his corner
of the forbidden streets.
His dog stares at him with hunger
while its body is quivering with the cold.
In his hat only a few pence lay there,
as he pleads for a few more pennies
to give his stomach a rest from the pain
of starvation.

The destitute beggar sits on his corner
of the forbidden streets.
His bewildered life is now getting worse.
All he has is a scrawny cloth to call his clothes
and his only friend is his dog.
They sit there and look at each other
with care and affection.
They forget about the poor place they are in.

Kirsty Hill (12)
Mascalls School

Autumn

Autumn is arriving,
Trees are getting bare.
Leaves are falling,
Through the cold air.
Nights drawing nearer,
Rain is all around,
So snuggle together,
Till summer comes around.

Abbie Collins (11)
Mascalls School

A Cat's Life

In the night cats are out,
In bushes and bins that's what it's about.
Who cares if they're white, black or grey,
They go inside to have food and play.

Having fish, chicken or milk,
Washing their fur until it's like silk.
Cats always make friends,
Just before every day ends!

Emma Shrimpton (13)
Mascalls School

Josephine

One day I saw a horse
It was a big horse of course
It ate some grass on a summer day
And it was the merry month of May.

I went to Isis to get some food
But Lucy said, 'Now don't be rude.'
Miss Hopkins was there as well
And she said, 'Look, where's its bell?'

Josephine was very sad
And the horse just got so mad
It ate some hay and got a pain
And then it began to rain.

When the rain had stopped its fall
We all went out to play with a ball
The sun came out and shone on us
And then we went to get the bus.

Josephine Shaw (12)
Meadows School

Feelings

I can't even speak about it
The way I feel
There's always conflict,
Between everyone

All I hear, shouting and crying
I see people running and hiding
When I ask what is wrong
All they do is sing a song

When I'm sad I sit alone
So I can think in a different zone

When I'm angry
I take deep breaths

I've got holes in the back of my door
Most of the time I sit on the floor

When I'm sad I drift away
Maybe I'll come back a different day.

Ashley Lockyer (15)
Meadows School

War Poem

The war is very sad and lonely
they cry out for their suffering and pain.
This family has lost a loved one
other people lost their son.
The cities are torn apart.
Their homes are burned down
and bombed down.
They are now homeless people
now living in despair and hunger.
They wish they would just wake up
and wish it was not true.
They now know that the world
will never be the same again.

Tanya McCarthy (14)
Meadows School

School Rap

In the unit Pauline's cool.
When she beats us all at pool.
Hazel is good when she comes in
She can make her tongue reach down to her chin.

Martin's cool - he's so tall
He's the king of basketball.

Eddie's joined the crew, he's so cool
He's started teaching in the school.

Miss Hopkins stresses when we lose
But when we win she brings the booze.

Mr Price is the man
If we work, there is no ban.
When we want him always ready
That's why we say, 'Price is steady.'

David Killick (13)
Meadows School

Anger

Angry feelings make you feel blue
They're not very nice to people around you.
They hurt,
Like a *knife* through your gut,
Like a *bee sting* in your arm,
They make you laugh, they make you cry
But when people cheer you up
They hide away till the next time you feel
Angry
They
Come
Back
Out.

Aaron Peters (15)
Meadows School

Anger Is . . .

Anger is a bully, who always cusses my mum,
Anger is someone who would call me scum,
Anger is a dog tied to a tree,
Anger is a zoo, animals should be free,
Anger is a baby dying, watching that baby in pain,
Anger is enough to turn someone insane.

Anger makes me angry when people lie,
Anger makes me angry when people die,
Anger is a hunter chasing a fox,
Anger is a family living in a box,
Anger is the news to see someone is dead,
Anger hurts, you can only see red.

Anger is to see birds get shot,
Anger is horrible it makes me feel hot,
Anger is when someone would steal,
Anger is the pain that will never heal,
Anger is a knife, blood up the wall,
Anger is the person who acts like a fool.

Anger is a sick person, who looks at people in a different way,
Anger won't go it will always stay,
Anger gets in your soul and your brain,
Anger is a country where children get the cane,
Anger isn't something God can hold,
But anger can always be controlled.

Allan Cole (14)
Meadows School

Empathy

Sometimes I feel good
Sometimes I feel bad
Sometimes I feel sad
Sometimes the feeling I get
From my feelings, confuses me so much
I feel nothing.

Ann-Marie Telfer (14)
Meadows School

Angry

Sometimes I feel angry
Angry because of racists.
The hatred people shout, 'Coon.'
It makes my insides woon.

Angry because of a little twelve-year-old girl
Standing on the corner waiting for sex.
Angry when people don't listen to me,
Angry when I bully people.
Angry when I have rows with my mum and dad,
Angry with myself.

Angry when I can't do my work,
Angry when I can't get my own way,
Angry when I make people I care about sad.

Angry when people spill blood,
Angry when people are in pain.
Angry when I walk in a shop and everyone stares,
Thinking I'm gonna steal,
Thinking that's real,
They don't know how I feel.

Angry when my friends are hurt,
Angry when I get excluded from school to school.
Angry when I'm angry.

Angry with the world,
Angry when people die.
Angry when I feel the world is gonna fry.

This is the world today,
Too much pain, won't go away.
This is my prayer,
What am I gonna say?
Let's make it a better day,
It's all gonna be Nightmare's way.

Nathan Lahrar (13)
Meadows School

Today

Tomorrow they say
Never comes.
It's always today
But with a bit of luck
I will feel better
Than yesterday.
Now I think
I'll go out to play
And have a good day.

Luke Dorey (14)
Meadows School

My New School

I feel good
I am doing OK
At my new school.
I am learning things
I thought were gone.
My chance has come
To prove to all
I can again stand tall.

Kieran Grant (14)
Meadows School

Bad Feelings Of War

The people at war,
Must have feelings no more,
We can only hope,
That these people will cope,
For there is only one world,
That we need to keep calm,
So no more innocents,
Will come to any harm.

Lee Mackay (15)
Meadows School

Crying And Dying

I'm crying and dying
Within my soul
I just can't let go
I fight myself every day
But I don't know why
Is it that I am scared?
Is it that I am running away
From myself and my life?
But nobody will let me give up
Thank God.

Karl White (15)
Meadows School

My Coffin Of Death

Life ended yesterday,
When I came to this place,
I've lost my soul
And the eyes from my face.

Bombs drop each second,
I've nowhere to hide,
I hear people screaming,
My age, I shouldn't have lied.

The death toll is mounting,
An epidemic is near,
My best friend was in the front line,
I wish he was still here!

O Lord, won't you help us?
I miss my daughter and my wife, Beth,
I'm afraid of dying,
Dying and being buried in this coffin of death.

Nathalie Gunn (15)
Minster College

Soldier Of War

There was a young soldier who went to war,
He started a fight to settle a score.

The young soldier went to fight,
His bravery like that of a knight.

He pushed through the enemy lines,
To stop their terrible crimes.

The gas masks were put to the test,
But there was no hope for the rest.

The bombs were a terrible sound
As the houses were put to the ground.

The buildings became dust,
The bridges turned to rust
And the birds never made a sound,

Many months have now passed,
The war over at last.

The birds start to sing
So let the bells now ring

And the people will join together.
It's now peace at last
No more bombs to blast
It's quiet in our land forever.

Emma Mason (13) & Lucy Parish (14)
Minster College

Laura

L aura is my name,
A nswering back is my game,
U nique for my own style,
R unning, I haven't done that in a while
A nd I was such a pain
    That's me!

Laura Gregory (13)
Minster College

War Of 1916

It was 1916, I remember so clearly,
Friends and family were missed dearly.
I was in first line, you don't know how much I shook,
The amount of courage that it took.

When war began I was shocked to see,
All those soldiers coming for me.
Guns were aiming, swords held high,
I wish I could have left and said bye-bye.

Shot in the leg, hit on the arm,
I cried so loud, I couldn't stay calm.
I was carried in the first-aid room,
Escaping from all that doom.

As I'm writing this, I'm in hospital,
Friends and family, I wish they'd call,
So now's the time to end this poem,
Goodbye, goodbye.

Claire Whitaker (14)
Minster College

My First World War Poem

Think of man and all the world
Say over and over again hearing bullets hurled
The screaming, the pain
Bullets, bombs and all just from one plane.

Whatever happened to singing birds?
All we hear now is the army in herds
Shouting and shouting by the thousands
Ambulance and fire engine sirens.

The peace and tranquility so far away
Dead bodies of war men lay
So obscured this war we lean and sway
One day all will be done
The clearance of dust so the sun would have shone.

Jamie McCombie (15)
Minster College

Front Line Fighting

I'm fighting a war on the front line
To live or to die, the decision is mine
I fight for my country, my family and all
Now I wait for headquarters to call.

The fighting begins at nine o'clock
The soldiers sail away from the dock
As the soldiers near the land
The colonel is shot in the hand.

The war has now begun
Trust me, it's not fun
We're counting the cost
As each life is lost.

We reach the war's end
And look for lost friends
Now there are a few more widows
But all we can do is pray for our heroes.

Brian Thain (13)
Minster College

War

He stands defiantly above the heath,
Scanning the battlefield for the enemy,
He sends his men to certain death.

Bullets flying above their heads,
They all take cover behind the buildings,
There they wait, ready to pounce.

They all jump up and run towards enemy lines,
Men and colleagues dropping like flies,
We all jump over the enemy walls and start the killing spree.

Daniel Goodwin (14)
Minster College

Why?

Why is it called a war?
Why do we ignore the law?
Why is there fighting
Whenever someone sees a sighting?

Why is there hate and violence?
Why is there blood and bone?
Why do we fight for a piece of bloody land
Only for it to be thrown?

Why is it called war?
First WW1, then WW2.
Why do we call it a world war
When all the world's not fighting?

I sit up in my room wondering
Why is there war?
Only I never find a reason
So I'm left asking . . .

Why?

Kirsty Elmes (15)
Minster College

Hallowe'en

Pumpkins, pumpkins, lighting up the street,
Pumpkins, pumpkins, hope I get some treats.
Pumpkins, pumpkins, I've got a scary mask,
Pumpkins, pumpkins, so you'd better run fast.

Monsters, monsters, roaming the streets,
Monsters, monsters with their big, hairy feet.
Monsters, monsters, I'm not scared of you,
Monsters , monsters, you have not got a clue.

Luke Brown (13)
Minster College

World War I

The battle has just begun,
The world is in terror,
What shall we do?
Stay at home worrying!
Or be there,
Be there helping our country.
Help them!
Because Britain needs you.
The bombs are exploding,
Exploding in our faces.
Our dead, cold bodies fall
To the hard, dirty ground.
We fall in shame,
We wonder
Could we have done more for our country?
They're shouting *'Bombs away'*.
It's too late,
The war has ended,
We've won.

Stacey Norris (14)
Minster College

Holding On

War is anger in people's faces,
War is sadness in people's hearts,
War is evil in people's eyes,
War is frightening in people's minds,
War means losing people you love,
Homes that you built,
Happiness that you created.
So ask yourself, what is the point of war?
And remind yourself of the people,
Homes that you will lose forever!

Charlotte Gath (13)
Minster College

My War!

This is my war!
Cold and damp,
Blood everywhere.

This is my war!
Friends dying,
Explosions, bullets
Flying everywhere.

This is my war!
The sounds of screams,
The smell of fear,
This was everywhere.

This is my war!
The sound of victory,
Sound of relief,
That was everywhere.

Nicholas Miles (14)
Minster College

The Fight In The War

Soldiers marching
Marching off to war
People fighting
Guns firing
Bombs exploding
People dying
In the war.

Men, women, children
All sad and crying
Houses destroyed
Alone and scared
Scared of dying.

Jeydon Fletcher (14)
Minster College

War Poem

Standing on the front line
Teeth chattering
Knees shaking
I don't want to be here
None of us do.

I'm gonna lay my gun down
I'm tired, I ache
My stomach's churning
I don't want to be here
None of us do.

Two bodies lying next to me
They didn't want to be here
None of us did
Two bodies wasted
I'm swallowing hard
They didn't want to be here
None of us do.

Months passing like days
My eyes are heavy and ache
Too scared to close them
Missing the smells of England
Bang!
Two more bodies down
I don't want to be here
None of us do.

Carly-Louise Fagg (14)
Minster College

War Poem

There are explosions going off everywhere, bodies scattered all over the ground. Soldiers without arms and legs. The wind is bitter cold with sand and dust flying around everywhere. The air smells of smoke and there are always bombs going off. My face is covered in sweat, my hands in oil and feet in sand. I am nervous of dying and leaving behind my family. I am scared!

Tara Chapman (13)
Minster College

The Front Line

This is me
This is my time
I am on the front line
Beware of ambush
I never thought it would be like this
The trenches filled with crying.

My life is in danger
I am a soldier
My friends go
Only some return, not all
Life is horror
I do not sleep
I only weep.

I think of life
Guns and bombs
Home is where I want to be
Warmth and food
You read the paper
Of me on the front line
Is this a sign?

Chloe Bates (14)
Minster College

Alone

Fires are the sounds I hear,
Wire is the thing I fear,
Clay is the thing I taste,
Corner is the place I waste,
What is that I see right there?
Blood all going everywhere.
Where are Mom and Papa?
Where are sis and brother?
Where am I, in the sky?
I'm all alone, so please don't cry.

Kasi Richardson (13)
Minster College

But Why?

In the middle of the night
When people walk in the light
We sit and pray that we will see the sky one day
All tied up in rope
When we sit and hope
That one day the war will be over
But why?

We sit in the dark
With just water and bread
When people are in the light
We just sit tight
Footsteps coming up the stairs
We sit and hope
It's the army to set us free
But why?

We think about the times we were free
We sit and wonder will it ever end
All the sounds of war and pain
We sit and wonder
But why?

Wesley Connor (14)
Minster College

Soldiers Dead

Soldiers dead
Shot in the head
Skull full of lead
'Goodbye,' he said.

Please no more!
Young men lost in the war
There is no cure
For the bodies on the floor.

Mothers dressed in black
Their sons are not coming back!

Adam Wilson (15)
Minster College

Victims

Damp,
    vomit,
        blood and smoke.
            I slouched through sweaty trenches
            My lungs filled with smoke.
           Limbs dead,
            Heart pounding,
             Guns start,
              Guts explode,
             Screaming,
            Yelling,
             Crying
              Bleeding
             to
                  death.

I wonder if Christmas will ever reach me . . .

Carla Feist (13)
Minster College

I'm Against The War

People go to war
They don't know how long for
They are scared for people who cared
I'm against the war.

All this fighting
All this hurting
I can see why people are dying
I'm against the war.

Bombs are exploding
Bodies are aching
People are worrying
I'm against the war.

Charlotte Rowe (14)
Minster College

War Poem

Hundreds of explosions every hour,
The shells coming all around,
I waited to see if one had my name on it.

I'm hungry, been living on rations,
The water is dirty, it doesn't taste too nice.
There I sat on the hill,
With a sniper and a licence to kill.

On the hill were seven other snipers shooting for their lives,
We shot down hundreds between us.
I had killed quite a few, they were lining up in a queue.
My conscience had got the better of me,
Down went one of the snipers, then two, three, then four.
Just me and three comrades left,
We listened to the radio that day,
We had won the war and Hitler was dead.

I had a feeling in me that I had done a bad thing,
I think I'll do something stupid
But I won't live to forget it.
Commit suicide I will.
Farewell my friends.

Matthew Gearing (13)
Minster College

Exit Wounds

I'm sitting here on my own,
People screaming, 'Take me home!'
Bullets passing, tanks around,
Get down on the grubby ground.
Blood is here, blood is there,
Blood is just everywhere.
Will people see the real right,
Why we're here to kill and fight?

Ross Allwright (16)
Minster College

War Poem

It was time for me to go out,
onto the battlefield of doom.
Most of us were hungry and thirsty,
but we had to carry on.
We all hope it's over soon.

The terror as we have to kill,
the horror of the sight.
I keep thinking of me in my bed,
hoping I will wake up,
wishing that I might.

I hurt all over,
the dirt on my face.
Bodies on the floor dying,
crying with the pain.
I hope, I hope,
I don't have pain to gain.

The confusion of us all,
of attacking
and bombs that are flying.
People bleeding,
people wondering
why it had come to this.

We have won,
us the heroes.
Our duty is done,
we have won.

Stephanie Collins (13)
Minster College

The Soldier

Shooting, shouting, is all I hear,
My hair's on end as I shake with fear.
Soldiers dying with bleeding wounds,
Let's hope paramedics get here soon!
Revenge, aggression, that's why we attack,
All we have to do is watch our back!
Terror, hurt, is what we all feel,
I can't wait for my next hot meal!
Full of guns, blood and army,
What was this meant to be?
Urine, vomit, everywhere,
Just as my clothes begin to tear.
When I shut my eyes, bodies are what I see,
Why did this all happen to me?
Blood, limbs, on my bed,
'I shouldn't be here,' says my head.
My pockets are full of ammunition,
But to fire them was my decision.
These all have families, why should I kill?
This isn't how I'd like to feel.
Nervous, worried and of course, lonely,
I used to be, oh so homely.
With my wife and our youngest baby,
Will I see them this Christmas?
The answer's a maybe!

Sarah Dear (13)
Minster College

Visions Of War

W onder, worry, windy
A ching, anger, ammunition
R iots, raids.

Amy Hall (14)
Minster College

Why?

Why did the war start?
Why hasn't the pain stopped?
Have the angels heard my cry
Or have they left me to die?
Wait, I see something.
It's the Major, dead.
Bang!
It's raining blood and bodies,
All I smell is the rotting bodies,
All I hear are the crying bodies.
A light I see.
Is it Heaven or is it Hell?
I am flying high in the sky.
I see someone,
Is it Satan or is it St Peter?
Maybe there is a God after all.
I hope so!

Robert Piper (13)
Minster College

A War Poem

Here I am, stuck in it all,
Around me bombs and mortars fall.
Around me all my family are dead,
The last thing Corporal Hunter said:

'Onward men, to victory,
The folk will honour us in story!
Come on men, keep it up!'
(That's when a shell blew him up.)

I lie here in this stinking trench,
I lie here in this awful stench.
The German forces will diminish,
Only then, this war will finish.

Thomas Hewitt (13)
Minster College

Scene Of War

The air raid siren goes,
Everyone knows,
The war will never end.
They are dying, we're not crying,
We're never going to stop,
Killing people as we climb a steeple,
When will it all end?

At the docks there are many shocks,
The boats are all destroyed.
On the deck, there a broken neck,
From fighting our British power.

An entire navy fighting for gravy
On their Yorkshire puds,
All who are good, we're the hood,
To all who stood in the British power.

The barmy army of the air,
Took flight without any care.
The Nazis came, killed a nun for fun
And we made sure they got done.

The war has ended,
The British extended
Their power for wealth and greed.
The Germans came to kill,
The British took with steed,
Now the Germans pay the bill
For trying to take the British power.

Aaron Clark (13)
Minster College

Will These Be Our Last Moments To Live?

As I climb into the tin can,
I start to shake.
We all start praying that we'll live to see our families again.
I can hear the sounds of gun shots near,
The terror in a child's screaming voice haunting me.

The smell of sweat, dust and smoke,
Fills the area that we sit in.
They're getting closer,
I feel scared, worried and sick.
We start to move,
Jolting forward,
Dust clouds fill the air like a gossamer curtain,
Leaving silhouettes of tanks and soldiers.
Will these be our last moments to live?

Hannah Payne (15)
Minster College

Life Never Lasts

The war had begun and no one knew
What was going to happen next.
It is a bad sport but
We're the best of the best.
My life is going to end,
It's not been great
But I have hundreds of dead bodies on my plate.
The smell is bad, not that good,
Lots of smoke from where I am stood.
The taste of food is worse than the war,
We were made to eat food that was raw.
Here it comes, I can see it coming,
The bomb is hurtling fast,
Now I am in a mushroom,
Life never lasts.

Cherie Simpson (13)
Minster College

What's Happened To Me?

Why me?
Why did I come?
I'm only sixteen.
I was too young.
Why did I come?
I wish I did not look older than I am.

All my unit dead.
Why am I alone?
I am sitting here with one arm.
How am I going to survive?
All my friends are gone.
Why, why did we come?

Now I can see a trench.
I start running there.
I hit the floor.
I can see Peter now with all my friends.

Paul Young (13)
Minster College

I Wonder

Blood and bodies all around me
as I pray for the war to end.
I can hear the gunshots
and I wonder when it's my time to go.

I wonder if we will survive
or whether we will die.
All I know is if I die
I will leave my family behind.

I know my family will always be with me
So if I die
At least I will die for my country.

Natalie Crossley (13)
Minster College

The Dugout

I had three hours sleep last night,
Kept awake by the screaming bombs and cries of fear.
I daren't open my eyes for fear of the ugly sight,
Oh, what the hell am I doing here?

From one corner I heard an old man's groans,
From another, a young boy's stifled, lonely sobs,
As soldiers we fought like clones,
Risking our souls, our lives and counting it 'our job'.

I stank, hadn't washed or changed my clothes in days,
It was paradise for the rats, they loved our filth!
Never-ending explosions caught us unawares,
Boom! I saw the fire blaze.

Wearily I rose and tried to rouse the others,
I stepped outside and that's when it happened.
The bomb flew past - smashed the dugout
And all inside to smithers.

Lizzie Martin (15)
Minster College

A Poem To The Great War

The people at home said,
'This war will be over by Christmas.'
For some it was
This war has been going on for years.

I thought this war was a glory war,
But all I see is death and destruction.
And all I hear are guns and cannons firing and exploding.
What have we done to God to deserve this?

Death and destruction because of one country,
Their armies attack, we defend.
They fight for domination,
We fight for freedom.

Michael Batchelor (13)
Minster College

Death's Pass

The greenness of the air,
Goes through my body
Like a sharp knife piercing my flesh.
My throat's dry.
The air is poison,
But it's too late for my life.

Beside me I see men falling,
No more do they cry.
No more do they hold a gun
To take someone's life,
But lie not moving, not speaking,
Just resting till they speak to the judge in the sky.

Fiona West (13)
Minster College

A Dark Day

A dark day as people march
To their deaths
As people fight to save our
Souls.
They fight but we remember
What they did.
Think . . . think of what they did
They died for us!
Could you do it? Could you
Leave your home, your mum,
Your dad, brother or sister?
They died so we could
Live!

Rebecca Penman (16)
Minster College

What's Going On?

The blood dripping down my leg
People are here, about to beg
There's shooting here, shooting there
People are dead everywhere.

Politicians lying and people dying
Why do we fight and kill?
Children hurt and see them crying
They are shooting above the hill.

A child just died, I am so sad
The war has never been this bad
I'm here with a person's who's dead
I just want to get in my bed.

All they're doing is pointing the gun
Then all I think about is my mum
I always say to them don't run
It will be all over and done.

Please, please don't give us more
Don't want it to end in a roar
Just end this rotten war
So I can knock on my own front door.

Aaron Gray (15)
Minster College

Megs

There was a centipede called Megs,
She only had ninety-nine legs.
Everyone would take the mick,
They said, 'Hey, you're missing a stick.'
Whenever she went for a walk in the park,
There would always be a lark.
She thought she would be cool if she took drugs,
Megs became a very sick bug.
She slowly and painfully died,
Everyone cried and said, 'Goodbye.'

Craig Allen (13)
Minster College

The Disturbance Of War

What I see
Is what I don't want to be
I will be free
When I have a cup of tea.

When I cover at night
I think of my lover
All bright.

The pace I run
Is a place for a gun
I am man
With no frying pan.

I'm always in the shade
Where my tan will fade.

In the corner of the night
I fear I will have to fight.

Omer Mertdogdu (15)
Minster College

D-Day

As the drawbridge went down
Our first platoon was shot down.
This was no flamboyant day
For it was the day of all days.

As our flag stood well and proud
We took them Jerries right to the ground.
We crouched and sneered in the bomb hole
To shoot our enemy one by one and all.

For I knew I would not stay alive,
But to fight for my country
Even though I would die.
My last words would be that I died for England,
That's why I died.

Carl Carolan (13)
Minster College

The Volcano

I am strong and large
Waiting, waiting
I feel a burning in the pit of my stomach
A rumbling, thundering

I feel something coming out from my mouth
Leaking, leaking
Sliding down making layers on my skin
Crunching, crackling

Nearly at the bottom of my body
Sliding, sliding
Flooding all the floors and places
Shouting, screaming

Slowly things start to change shape
Crumbling, crumbling
Nothing else to be seen, just a lumpy floor
Splash, slob sparks so special

The layers have stopped going
Still, still
It becomes solid and hard
Frozen, stable

The place was calm
Silent, silent
There was quiet through the skies and seas
Cold, stiff

I feel so empty inside myself
Blank, blank
My stomach starts to burn again
Heat, warmth

I have to do this every twenty years.

Vinson Lee (15)
St Mary & St Joseph's School, Sidcup

Soldier Story

Seeing you going to the wars
Out of the house
And you're gone.

Makes me feel guilty
I might have lost the most important thing in my life
Like losing my heart.

I am always waiting for you
To knock on the door and I'll open it
But maybe you won't come back.

What I may be losing is a son of gold
All that is left for me to remember
Is your bravery and courage.

Seconds, minutes, hours, days, weeks, months and years
Have come and passed
And you haven't come back.

I am sitting on my wheelchair
Growing grey hair
And not going anywhere, not without you.

I am waiting for the dark
My time to finish
So that we can be together.

Don't worry my son
Wait for me
I will soon be with you.

Irene Muiruri (11)
St Mary & St Joseph's School, Sidcup

But You Didn't!

Remember when we went to the theatre
And I dropped a cup of tea on your lap?
I thought you would scream at me . . .
But you didn't!

Remember when I shouted at you
Because you broke a cup?
I thought you would leave me . . .
But you didn't!

Remember when I got drunk at a party
And started flirting with other men?
I thought you would walk away . . .
But you didn't!

There are lots of things I had to say sorry for
And I never thought it mattered . . .
But it did!

Georgina Lampen (13)
St Mary & St Joseph's School, Sidcup

The Wind

As the wind blows the trees
On your cheek a gentle breeze
As the leaves whirl around
Then softly fall to the ground.

As the wind blows the flowers
With its gentle cunning powers
As the wind makes waves in the sea
Everything is swaying as gently as can be.

But now everything is still
Even the grass on the hill
The wind I'm sorry to say
Has gone off another way.

Nadine Ijewere (11)
St Mary & St Joseph's School, Sidcup

First World War

It went on for four years,
Most of it was tears.
I had my friends and foes,
Also my highs and lows.

I made my fist clench,
As I went into the trench.
I felt fear,
As the enemy came near.

The years didn't go fast,
But it finished at last.
As I came home I heard a cheer,
As I came in to shore it got so near.

Was it over for good?
And I thought it could.
Did the First World War
Bring us any law?

Anthony Manzi (13)
St Mary & St Joseph's School, Sidcup

Boom!

Boom! The battle had finally started
Days of waiting were over.
Hearts were beating faster
As we crawled through the mud and clover

Boom! A shell exploded near me
I thought my time had come
But God was with me that day
It was others who were killed by the bomb

Boom! For hours the battle raged
Daylight turned to night
On both sides men were dying
What reason this bloody fight.

Nichola Mitchell (13)
St Mary & St Joseph's School, Sidcup

New School

When I came to this new school
I had to go to the hall.
The first time I came to learn
I knew that friends I had to earn.

When I came I wore a tie
And I saw some kids walking by.
I could not believe I was in Year 7
I wanted to die and go to Heaven.

I finally made a couple of friends
But we found out we needed pens.
I had to meet the head of year
I sat in my chair and shook in fear.

Eugen Sagalla (11)
St Mary & St Joseph's School, Sidcup

Dinosaurs

Dinosaurs can be big
Dinosaurs can be small
They come in different sizes
But it doesn't matter at all.

Dinosaurs are ferocious
Some are hostile too
Some are herbivores
But some are predators.

Dinosaurs rip
Dinosaurs chew
Dinosaurs bite
And there's others too.

Joshua Bonhill Smith (11)
St Mary & St Joseph's School, Sidcup

All About The Loner

I stand alone in the corner of the playground
And everyone walks past and laughs
Also they point at me and that upsets me.

I have only one friend, his name is Matthew
My name is Mark
He sits in the corner with me sometimes
We have fun with each other
I don't have fun with my brother.

Most of the time he goes and plays
That upsets me too, most of the days
My teachers say go and play with them
I've only asked one person, his name is Ben.

He said yes but then went off and left me
But Mark came over and asked me if I was OK
And I said to him leave me be.

So he went away and I wished I hadn't told him to go away
Because I was bored
Please make people like me, please Lord.

My teacher told everyone to be nice to me.
Everyone was and I started to play with people
And I felt much happier because I had lots of friends.

Danielle Sullivan (11)
St Mary & St Joseph's School, Sidcup

Goodbye

So it's goodbye
What more can I say?
It's bon voyage
Today is not a happy day
The children are gone
The classroom is bare
But yet one student is still there.

Deborah Obaseki (11)
St Mary & St Joseph's School, Sidcup

I Wish I Was A Pirate

I wish I was a pirate
Their lives are full of fun
If anyone annoys them
They shoot them with their gun
Or cut their throat, or hang them up
To dangle from the mast
Or simply throw them overboard
To drown and breathe their last.

I wish I was a pirate
I'd sail the ocean blue
There'd be so many sword fights
And exciting things to do
I'd dig for buried treasure
On an island in the sun
Until I found a hoard of gold
And jewels by the ton.

I wish I was a pirate
But what if I was caught
And tried for all my crimes - and *hanged!*
Oh! What a horrid thought
I think I'm going to change my mind
About the pirate's life
I'd rather raise a family
With children and a wife!

Christopher Collinge (12)
St Mary & St Joseph's School, Sidcup

I Am

I am a chilled out cool blue
I am a ray of sunshine which glitters in the sky
I am a Nike pair of football boots
Which covers every inch of a football pitch
I am a nice, cosy, comfortable settee
The Premiership is me, it has lots of action and fun
I am a hard red with lots of crunch.

Charlie Ward (11)
St Mary & St Joseph's School, Sidcup

Why Did . . . ?

Why did the animals escape from the zoo?
Is it because they had nothing to do,
Or because the zoo keeper got sued?

Why did they trample all over the town?
Is it because they wanted to see a clown,
Or because there was so much sound?

Why did they eat the fat, bald man?
Is it because . . . well, they ate him anyway,
So everybody ran?

Why did they demolish the school?
Is it because they didn't think it was cool?
So the teachers started screaming, 'You broke all the rules!'

Why did the keeper capture the zoo?
When all the children started crying, 'Boo hoo.'

The zoo was back and that was that.
The zoo was quiet, nobody came.
'Miaow,' purred a cat,
So why did it happen?

Katie Gianakakis (11)
St Mary & St Joseph's School, Sidcup

A Terrible Thing

Conflict is such a terrible thing,
It takes lives,
It takes love,
With one swing of a sword, one swing,
Or the trigger of a gun,
It takes lives,
It takes love,
It takes a father from his son.

Matthew Foy (13)
St Mary & St Joseph's School, Sidcup

Monster Under The Stairs

Walking past the staircase I hear a crash
The noise I heard got even louder with a bash
That night I walked past with lots of fear
I felt a cold breeze very, very near.

Crash, bang - lots of noise
Walking past it sounds like a gang of boys
Now I'm scared of my own stairs
When I open the closet I'm full of scares.

At night when I need a drink I bring a torch
The monster could be lurking in the porch
I know it's bright pink with yellow spots
And its hair is blue and full of knots.

Crash, bang - lots of noise
Walking past it sounds like a gang of boys
Now I'm scared of my own stairs
When I open the closet I'm full of scares.

I heard it shouting, 'My name is Spot'
But this monster Spot has scared me a lot
When it knows I'm scared it laughs
And runs quickly past me leaving a draught.

He is big and noisy and a sly creature
So basically he has a very big feature
He eats our shoes and steals our toys
And in an evil voice he says, 'I eat little boys.'

He runs like a rocket in the air
But believe me he is such a scare
He has hairs coming out his ears
When he gets his way believe me he cheers.

At night I hear the drip drop
He drinks from the tap and gurgles at the top
My mum says I'm going mad
But I'm not and if I was I would be glad.

I haven't seen him for a while
So I put on a happy smile
He must have gone to another house
'Yes,' I yelled, 'he isn't at ours!'

Stacey Rump (11)
St Mary & St Joseph's School, Sidcup

Jack Frost

Snowflakes appear to dance by night,
They often surprise you with delight.
The rain will wash your fears away,
Jack Frost's bright light is here to stay.

The blossom appears to bloom by day,
Newborn lambs snuggle in the hay.
The rain will wash your troubles away,
Jack Frost's sparkle is fading, we pray.

The sun awakes you early in the morning,
It's burning glare has everyone dawdling.
The rain won't wash your tears away,
Jack Frost's shimmer has gone astray.

Gusty winds in the afternoon,
Sweeping leaves away with a broom.
The rain will wash your troubles away,
Jack Frost's bright light is back to play.

Winter, spring and autumn too,
The cold white lurks behind the dew.
Only summertime can we escape,
From Jack Frost's cruel and icy fate.

Sian Ciara Seymour (11)
St Mary & St Joseph's School, Sidcup

The Night Before . . .

The night before my first day at school,
Silly me, I cried like a fool.
My mum tried to convince me it wouldn't be so bad,
But still I couldn't sleep, my nerves were driving me mad.

2am and I still lay awake,
Why, oh why for goodness sake?
I wanted to be alert on my first day,
But still my fears wouldn't fade away.

I tried counting sheep,
But this didn't work.
I could hear the clock ticking,
It was driving me berserk.

All sorts of thoughts filled my mind,
Would I keep up with the work?
I didn't want to fall behind.

I chewed my nails,
I twiddled my thumbs.
I couldn't stop thinking about what was to come.

7.30am and I woke to the sound
Of my mum pottering around.
'Time to get up,' I heard her call,
'If you don't get up now, you'll be late for school!'

I arrived at school with Lily, my friend,
I felt excited in the end.
I wondered what the teachers were like,
Would they be strict? Would they be nice?

My day at school really flew by,
All those nerves, why, oh why?
My day was great after all,
And I couldn't wait for my next day at school.

Georgina Heneghan (11)
St Mary & St Joseph's School, Sidcup

School Fights

I had a fight
It wasn't funny
He's stole my money

I was told to stick up for myself.
Fists were flying
And he started crying.

I said, 'Sorry'
He said, 'Sorry'
And the teacher said, 'You can go then.'

The boy's name was Tim
He's somewhat dim
But he's my best friend, now.

Funny how things turn out.

Sam Leonard (13)
St Mary & St Joseph's School, Sidcup

Summer Holidays

Sand beaches,
Blazing hot sun,
Crystal clear sea,
Like a sheet of glass,
Rocks to climb on,
Like a tree in the sea,
Staying up late,
Life can be great,
Playing in the pool,
Acting like a fool,
Flumes so fast,
Like a bullet from a gun,
Summer holidays,
Oh life can be fun.

Ben Faurie (12)
St Mary & St Joseph's School, Sidcup

Monster Poem

Down in the dungeon lives you know who,
It is the monster that is made out of goo.
Do you know what?
Some people think it's murky,
But I just think it is funky.
It moves so slow and always eats coal,
It is the monster of Bugdoo.

It growls all night and does not fight,
Its looks are like it is bad,
But it's always still like it is dead,
Do you know it's name?
It is Kane.
It's as big as mongrel dogs,
But speaks like three little frogs.
It is the monster of Bugdoo.

No one knows about these creatures,
But I've surely seen all of its features.
It lives where it's cold,
And now you've been told.
It is the monster of Bugdoo.

Michelle Besa (11)
St Mary & St Joseph's School, Sidcup

Appearance

She felt the persuasive strings cut into her arms and legs
You see she had another fight with the girls at school today
I heard her frantic; distressed with desperate screams and begs.
Once they had finished with her, I watched her lay,
When she saw those bullies coming she should have just fled.
Once I saw them finish with her I felt completely dismayed.
Why treat her like this? Was it something she said?
I watched as she was pulled this way, that way,
I wondered what revulsion and loathing for them,
Was going through her head?
This would be another one of those rainy days.

Heidi Pullig (13)
St Mary & St Joseph's School, Sidcup

Monster Poem

Monster, monster, where can he be?
Under my bed or under the sea?
When they run the monster chases,
He usually gets his food.
My monster's name I cannot say,
Because he lives in the dark day.
He eats whenever he can,
Soon the world will be gone.

Monster, monster, where can he be?
He is big and cold,
He is very scary and leery.
Crunch, crunch, the world will crack,
He lives in the deep, dark woods.
He's cold-blooded,
He kills people and eats them whole,
So whenever you see him,
You will see a skeleton hanging out of his mouth,
Monster, monster, where can he be?

Shaun Egan (11)
St Mary & St Joseph's School, Sidcup

The Sea

I like the sea and the sea likes me,
I like the waves as they chase me.
The waves roll in and the waves roll out,
But if I'm not careful they'll knock me about.

The waves came in all fluffy and white,
But why do they look so different at night?

As the waves come in they make such a sound,
Sometimes they even lift me off the ground.

I like the sea and the sea likes me,
Would you like to be at the sea with me?

Rachel Johnston (11)
St Mary & St Joseph's School, Sidcup

The Weather!

I'm the sun I shine all around
I give you suntans, I can burn you
I shine on the puddles to disappear
Now everyone comes out
Because I'm the sun.

I'm the whooshing, pushing, shooshing wind with coolness
I sweep away the leaves with a blow of air
I storm down the river
I blow in and out from the shore
Because I'm the wind.

I'm the rain which always drips down
I can flood all around
I come through your tap
I run your bath
Because I'm the rain.

Adam Hardie (11)
St Mary & St Joseph's School, Sidcup

Monster Poem

This is a monster that lives underground,
all through the day it makes no sound.
Be careful in the day, but even more in the night,
if it comes near you you'll be in for a fright.
When it is hungry, it's bloodthirsty for men,
it thinks you are big enough, when you are ten.
When the moonlight shines, its blood runs cold,
an experienced being, for a long 100 years old.
Its teeth are enormous, about the size of us,
its tail is magnificent, like a double decker bus.
When it goes to its cave, it has to travel east,
when it arrives, it has a great big feast.
When the clock hits twelve, it gives out a cry,
then the wind changes, the boats crash by.
If I knew its name, if not don't blame,
this great big monster, that once came.

Alfie Clark (11)
St Mary & St Joseph's School, Sidcup

Whatever Goes Around Comes Around!

I've been there,
I've done that,
It just don't work . . .

I tell a teacher and they say ignore,
I do, I do . . .
But they do it more.

I'm in Year 9,
It comes to a point I can't take it anymore,
So I pay them back with crime.

I come to school to learn,
So what if I'm not thin . . .
So what if I'm not fat . . .
So what if I'm not your standard?

But nothing's good for you!

You criticise whatever,
Just to be the king of popular,

But hey, it's not funny,
People take it to heart.

So watch what you say,
So watch what you do . . .
Whatever goes around,
Comes around,
So it might hit you.

Cherrelle Morgan (13)
St Mary & St Joseph's School, Sidcup

Freedom

Lying in the darkness
Working day after day
I look into the sky
And see all my dreams float away.

When I see the children
Crying through the day
I think to myself
Can't this all go away?

Sometimes I think to myself
Why does this have to happen?
I know why I am in this mess
But I know it will not go away.

Why can't I be like everyone else
Because they have freedom?

Rebecca McCormack (12)
St Mary & St Joseph's School, Sidcup

Who Was There?

Adults forget when they were young
The times they had
The fun is gone
They may recall those special few
But most of them don't have a clue
When you are a teenager
Times are confusing
It's the stage in your life
When nothing's choosing
Everything's planned ahead
The day, the week, the wedding, the dead
Maybe not all those out there
Try not to stare
But you might find in life
No one cares
So look around at the ones who were there.

Jimmy Hicks (14)
St Mary & St Joseph's School, Sidcup

Monster Poem

It's as dark as a forest
It's as quiet as a pin drop
It never moves his position once it stops.

It watches you like an owl
It speaks with mimes
It moves within a minute.

Its eyes are as big as the Earth
Its wings stretch out to catch its prey
Its feet are nothing but claws.

Its teeth are as sharp as knives
Its face is as lumpy as a stone
What's his name?

No one knows,
But soon we will
When this monster returns.

Patricia Abidakun (11)
St Mary & St Joseph's School, Sidcup

Slavery Poem!

Separated from loved ones,
What shall I do?
My dreams is a nightmare,
That has finally come true.

Working hard day and night
In the fields, picking cotton
Till I'm rotten.
If we don't work we get whipped or killed!

No one cares so be prepared,
For when the end is here,
To meet my Lord, I will not fear.
Release, relief I will pray,
Then cotton fields are far away!

Rhianne Supple (12)
St Mary & St Joseph's School, Sidcup

The Monster Of The Dark

The monster of the dark
The way he moves and strolls,
He jumps around and lurks,
He lives in great big holes.

Who knows what he likes,
The frightening noise he makes,
His tummy sounds like a motorbike,
He takes people who he hates.

He looks like a hair ball
The hair of his body is thicker than his self
He rolls down the road like a football
He jingles like a bell.

He loves scaring people off their feet,
He jumps like a kangaroo,
The monster body has lots of healthy meat,
He's called a Nazaroo.

Ronnie Gleeson (11)
St Mary & St Joseph's School, Sidcup

Bed Monster

There is a monster under my bed
and the monster needs to be fed.

The monster only comes out at night
and does not like the light.

He is very big, grey and very fat,
he is so fat because he ate the neighbour's cat.

The monster is so hairy, he is terribly scary.
The monster likes to eat my clothes
and he tries to lick my toes.

The monster has got no name
and he is very tame!

Christopher Lynch (11)
St Mary & St Joseph's School, Sidcup

Swiss Roll Fight

Tonight my mum got really mad
And threw a Swiss roll at my dad

He flung to the floor with a graceful drive
For his age - 35

        My sister who is only 3
        Hurled two at him and one at me

        I said I wouldn't stand for that
        Aimed one at her but hit the cat

The cat jumped up like she'd been shot
And landed in the baby's cot

The baby quietly sucking her thumb
Now started wailing for her mum

        Mum ran to the cot ducking and diving
        But Dad launched a pie, it was really flying

        Mum turned to the left but with a scream
        Her whole face was covered in cream

She fell to the floor rolling and swearing
I ran off, Dad was staring

        Tonight my mum got really mad
        And threw a pie at my dad.

Conor Cooper (12)
St Mary & St Joseph's School, Sidcup

Me

I wish I knew where angels fly
I wish I knew why I'm so shy
I wish I knew why I'm so caring
I wish I knew where the sun really shines
I wish I knew why I'm so loved
But then it comes to me . . .
That's just *me!*

Rosie Major (11)
St Mary & St Joseph's School, Sidcup

Game On

The O² sign is blazing bright
Through the Stadium of Light
The Gunners verse the evil Devils
But nobody knows who will win.
Henry's on the ball and he scores a great goal,
Heads up lads, get ready to win.

Keano's running down the centre,
He's tackled by Paddy V.
He plays a good ball,
He's just great, he is cool.
Goal!
Now let's make it 3.

2-0 is the score, it's just getting better.
Man United are pants, they're as bad as the weather.
The crosses are flying and so are the tackles,
Oh, that one looked dirty,
As John O'Shea cackles.

The 90th minute is drawing nearer,
The result to this game is becoming clearer.
Man U score a goal but that will not matter,
2-1 is the score, all their dreams have been shattered!

Ciaran O'Mahony (11)
St Mary & St Joseph's School, Sidcup

The Garden

Walking down the garden is a dream for me,
Seeing all the flowers makes me happy and joyful
The colours stare back at me and I see
Butterflies, bees and frogs jumping at me.

I peer down the garden
And who should I see?
Mum calling me in for tea.

Christopher Loughlin (11)
St Mary & St Joseph's School, Sidcup

War Of Slaughter

In they ran to battle,
All guns a-blazing,
Screams here,
Screams there,
Soldiers being slaughtered.

In the fighters jets flew,
The bombs raining down,
Bloodshed here,
Bloodshed there,
Soldiers being slaughtered.

There the soldiers lay,
Some dead, some alive,
Suffering here,
Suffering there,
Soldiers had been slaughtered.

The soil red with blood,
Mounds full of body parts,
Destruction there for all to see,
Soldiers had been slaughtered.

The sun was beaming down,
Although it wasn't hot,
Surviving soldiers struggled to their feet,
And trudged away from battle.

Joshua Nwanazia (13)
St Mary & St Joseph's School, Sidcup

You Are Everything

You're my friend
My companion
Through good times
And bad.

You're my hero
My lover
Through tough times
And sad.

You're my smile
My joy
Through tears
And laughter.

You're my hero
My companion
Through good times
And bad.

I know you'll be there
Throughout the years
And I am grateful to you
For all that you do.

Stephanie Jaques (14)
St Mary & St Joseph's School, Sidcup

Being Free

Being free
Is the place I long to be.
Being free
Is what I long to see.
I want to be back with my family.

I want to have time to play,
I want to have friends.
I don't even know what friends mean.

I want to be free!

Sarah Jeffrey (12)
St Mary & St Joseph's School, Sidcup

Yesterday

Yesterday there was a child
Simple and mild
Playing and giggling
Was the only thing in his mind
Laughing and always yapping
Never giving up even when he's choking
Loves clowning
But hates it when someone is cloning

Yesterday there was a child
Simple and mild
Living his life
So perfect and liked
Problems were not very serious
And as they grew up, they became curious

Yesterday there was a child
Simple and mild
Time is running fast
Do you still remember the past?
In our lives we meet a lot of castes
Good or bad, remember them we must

Yesterday there was a child
Simple and mild
While we grew up, changes emerge out
From the times we only thought of lust
We now must consider what is just.

Georgia Lynne Mae Bocanog (16)
St Mary & St Joseph's School, Sidcup

Thugs In A Park

He was walking home slowly through a park,
There was plenty of time before it got dark.
When as quick as a flash they appeared,
Much older than him, one had a beard.
They started to yell, then push and pull,
Shouting and cussing, this was their rule.
Out-numbered and frightened he looked to break free,
But he was hit with a bat across his left knee.
He cried out in pain and tears flooded down,
His trembling face all battered and brown.
Not knowing what he could try next,
He thought of his phone to send a quick text.
But guessed they would not give him a chance,
They threw stones at his feet to make him dance.
About to give up and wish he was dead,
He put up his hands to cover his head.

Henry Sivell (14)
St Mary & St Joseph's School, Sidcup

Torment

A sea of bodies left behind,
As we trudge through our misery,
Tired and tormented by a fiery hell,
That destroyed our mind and body.

We were cold and weary,
Sick of sin in anguish,
Green fields have turned red with blood,
I lie crying in torment over the death that I have seen.

I see friend and foe die before my eyes,
Hell has fallen from the sky,
People crying, people dying,
My life as I know it will be changed forever!

Joseph Duggan (13)
St Mary & St Joseph's School, Sidcup

A Teenager

Questions travelling around my brain
confused . . .
Where to stand?
How to act? Adult or still a child?
What to feel?

Still on the arms of my parents
entering the world of puberty
getting ready to take the risks of life
curious of doing everything . . .

Chased by the shadows
of a child
influenced by the future

Staying in the middle
makes me mad
feeling the highs and lows
of life . . .

Can't wait to get
out of here . . .
hoping to have a good
future.

Rachelle Bocanog (14)
St Mary & St Joseph's School, Sidcup

I Am Free

I am free, I am free
I cannot believe I am free
I am not a slave anymore, never again
People have lost their freedom over me
White people are the slaves because they make us slaves
I am free because I found the magic place of freedom
Being free is wonderful
Being free you can enjoy life
Being free you can wait for another day
You will not go into a field, day or night.

Tim Masera (12)
St Mary & St Joseph's School, Sidcup

War!

Walking through the sea of dead bodies
Kicking them as they went
Wanting to go home
Like so many others.

They weren't scared of the bombs
Machine guns or bangs
They had heard it every day.

Some were blinded
Some were wounded
From this terrible war
They had to listen carefully
For any attack at all.

They could hear screams from all around
Of people getting shot
People just lying there
Waiting to die.

Trust me, war is not a good thing
People die or get hurt
Some die quickly
But some are left to
Rot.

Shauna McDonagh (13)
St Mary & St Joseph's School, Sidcup

Sound

What is that something that troubles the air?
Travelling earth-wise like waves
Waiting for someone, a victim to hear
Hoping that someone obeys.

Whirling, upsetting, vibrating the air
Desperately seeking attention
Throwing its power like a mischievous child
All it needs now is a mention.

Sam Edwards (11)
St Mary & St Joseph's School, Sidcup

The General Said

'Run, run!' the general said
As many a soldier died or bled
Bullets were zooming, guns were booming
And bombs were looming overhead.

'Fire, fire,' the general said
And many a soldier died or bled
Dirt tossed and turned in the air
Mixed with blood, skin and hair.

No one knew, but to fire
As bombs came down like a rain of fire
The bombs exploded, the guns reloaded
And the fear in our hearts our expression showed it.

Enemy to the left, enemy to the right
We must kill them with full-blown might
All disorientated, almost won
The battle was over, finished and done.

'Hooray, hooray!' the general said
As many a soldier laid still or was dead
Silence found the battlefield
When life laid down, tortured and killed
All was not over at their demise
The image lives on in my teary eyes!

Chris Pullig (13)
St Mary & St Joseph's School, Sidcup

Being Free

The courage of love,
The power to think,
The freedom to choose,
The ability to decide for myself,
The right to make good use of all that God has created
The master of all world itself.

Sinead Connolly (12)
St Mary & St Joseph's School, Sidcup

Love

Affection, amity
Courtship, delight
Liking, charity
Regard and might.

What I feel
And what I seal
Are boundaries
To what I know.

And there you are
Before me now
Like a saint sent
From Heaven above.

One look at you
Makes my heart thud
One thought of you
Makes my core wound.

Night and day
April, May
You wear a crown.

My soul yearns
For you
My thoughts lean
To you
What is it I desire?
What is it I sense?
That burns me up inside
Makes my knees go weak?

Could it be?
Couldn't be?
That what I feel here
Could be *love*.

Bose Bakare (13)
St Mary & St Joseph's School, Sidcup

A Vision Of War

The soldiers march forward,
All trembling with fear.
Each one of them thinking,
Why am I here?

They see the enemy,
They prepare to fight.
Their friends collapse,
They think, *what a terrible sight.*

Cries of pain
Is all that they hear.
A river of blood
Is all that they see.

The fear in their hearts,
The rage in their eyes.
You can't imagine
What it feels like.

Through the smoke
They see the bodies.
Thousands of them
All heaped on the floor.

It takes so many lives
All innocent ones.
The soldiers have died,
All far too young.

Laura Sugrue (13)
St Mary & St Joseph's School, Sidcup

Conflict Poem

Bang! I shuddered as the first gun went off,
It was pursued by about five more,
The smoke haunted me as I sprinted,
Soldiers followed me as we huddled for safety.
Bang! Bang! Bang!
Like old men with walking sticks along we went,
No escape, the cartridges had found way to us.

Away from harm's way,
I rotated my body,
My vision of the foe,
Was like an old lady who's had her cataract done!
I held my rifle and shot towards the enemy,
Bang! Bang! Bang!
No hope left for them as their corpses fell to the ground.

Silence broke out as we waited for the next explosion.
But there was none.
Was this the end? Had we won? Where had they all gone?
Like men waiting for pigs to fly, we knelt for ages.
Not wanting to turn the corner,
Just in case the enemy was awaiting.

As noble as men could be, we got up after some time,
We leaped for joy as we proudly walked past the bodies,
Of those we shot down,
Swimming in the enemies' blood.
As we walked along, we gave each other a little gleam.
Then out of nowhere, bang! Bang! Bang!
I fell into the river.

Jade Murphy (14)
St Mary & St Joseph's School, Sidcup

Shadow Of Death

Running in the shadow of death
The soldiers seemed to be hexed
Bullets sprayed into soldiers' chests
Sending them towards death
Young and old all the same
Dying in agonising pain

Bullets flew
Soldiers were falling
Wondering what had happened to their world
Soldiers crying
Soldiers dying
Engulfed in the flames of Hell they fell

Blood soaked the charred field
Where once children's merry laughter pealed
Bodies scattered everywhere
Bullet holes here and there
Young and old all the same
Dead with expressions of agonising pain
No soldiers lived
Lived to see
The grotesque aftermath of what had been

Bullets had flown
Soldiers had fallen
Wondering what had happened to their world
People had cried
People had died
Engulfed in the flames of Hell
Soldiers they fell
Pulled away from their beloved world.

Philip Streete (13)
St Mary & St Joseph's School, Sidcup

Moon

Think how it would be
To live in the moon and not here.
Imagine how it would be
To feel the silence and nothing to hear.
Think of how many times
You have seen that beautiful satellite,
And how many rhymes
You can do with that shiny planet.
Maybe you don't like the night,
In one of those holes, that are there
But imagine the beautiful sight
Of the big blue Earth.
How it would be, the trip
That goes through space
To get at a grip
Of one of those colourful aliens.
But on the very other side,
The moon is a traitor,
Because she tells us
That she has her own life,
And the poor bright sun
Giving his light to others
So it looks as if it runs
From sun, to moon, to Earth.
These are the two sides of the moon,
The dark and the bright,
This is how we see the moon
From here, as we look up to the sky.

Isabel Irarrázaval (13)
St Mary & St Joseph's School, Sidcup

Slavery

Slaves were treated really bad,
Made to feel so very sad,
Whipped and shot,
No bed or cot,
No wooden floor,
Not even a door.

Slaves were treated really bad,
Made to feel so very sad,
Picking cotton,
For men so rotten,
Starting work at seven,
Finishing way past eleven.

Slaves were treated really bad,
Made to feel so very sad,
Black women and men,
Children younger than ten,
Born in a shed,
Forced to work till they're dead.

Slaves were treated really bad,
Made to feel so very sad,
A dream of being free,
In a place they long to see,
Canada is the place,
That will put a smile back on their face.

Kelly Marrington (12)
St Mary & St Joseph's School, Sidcup

War

What's going on in the world today?
People going off to fight each day.
10,000 men and women alone,
Going off to fight in a destruction zone.
They set off heads held high,
Some come back with no limbs or eyes.

Spare a thought for the families left behind,
Worrying about loved ones going out of their minds.
10,000 men and women alone,
Going off to fight in a destruction zone.
But the people who start these terrible conflicts,
Should be locked up like murderous convicts.

Bullets flying everywhere, men dropping dead,
Cries of pain, a sea of red.
10,000 men and women alone,
Going off to fight in a destruction zone.
They come back battered and bruised,
Feeling unwanted and used.

Jenny Faurie (13)
St Mary & St Joseph's School, Sidcup

Conflict

C is for cruel and cruelty, daring in the name of war
O is for the orders that must be obeyed
N is for numbing to the sounds and deeds, the silence that breaks
 your soul, your back and your morale
F is for friendship that depravation and hardship bring
L is for longing for peace, family and home
I is for insufferable, no imagination can take you there
C is for cannon balls thundering through the air
T is for the torture of watching men being slaughtered!

All this spells conflict, the thing all soldiers must do and endure.

Noëleen Spiteri (13)
St Mary & St Joseph's School, Sidcup

Being Free

Being free is being away
From slavery
Being able to do
The things you want to do
Being able to say
The things you want to say
Being able to play
The games you want to play
Being free is sleeping
Without fear
Being yourself and nobody else's person
Being able to think
What you want
Being able to have the time
To stop and stare
Being able to have the time
To stop and care.

Tom Kelleher (12)
St Mary & St Joseph's School, Sidcup

Hallowe'en

Children dress up in different costumes,
Out to give people a fright,
Knocking on doors, collecting sweets,
And they're all feeling sick by the end of the night!

For some people Hallowe'en is like hell,
For kids it's something to look forward to,
Running around trying to be scary,
People find it a funny thing to do.

Older people have fun throwing eggs,
They look at it in a different way,
Spoiling it for the younger children,
They're ruining it at the end of the day.

Kieran McCarthy (13)
St Mary & St Joseph's School, Sidcup

Advice

I remember when I tried to steal, then I got caught
From then on I knew it was bad to steal
And now I'm living and how great I feel.

You don't want to be expelled from school
Because believe me, it's really not cool
Because people talk about you like you're a fool.

Make sure you work hard and concentrate
So in your future job you can even walk in late
If you work hard in school, you will get really paid
Then you can even buy a diamond spade.

So listen to the advice I have given to you
And work hard in school
    I seem to be lazy but it's not my fault.

Sesugh Angula (11)
St Mary & St Joseph's School, Sidcup

My Conflict Poem

Fights and arguments are all I hear
They do it all the time
Are they expecting a cheer?

Under my blanket I hide
Hiding away with my ted
Why did Daddy have to confide?
Why did he tell Mummy I said?

Glasses smashing
Doors slamming
Cupboards crashing

Day in and day out
They've forgotten about me
They used to call me a little scout
Dad is now going, who I can no longer see . . .

Ben Hudson (13)
St Mary & St Joseph's School, Sidcup

War Is Not The Answer

My stomach felt like crashing waves
It churned, it felt so coarse
My heart could not control the distress
As those friends I'd lost, was hard to accept and ever so agonising
But as we drew closer in
I see the shore so red and distraught
As I see dismembered parts drift by.

I began to feel a tear trickle down my cheek
My family I miss so much
Why did I come? I feel so weak
My head is spinning, it is not all good to fight for your country
It's unbearable to think of the state I could return in
You have to sit in a wheelchair and be stared upon.

Suddenly I felt myself be thrown through the air
As I descended back into the trenches
My worst thoughts were becoming reality
It was horrifying to look and see what damage had been done
Even if I go home in a fit state, I will still be paralysed
But as I close my eyes all I could see was the disturbing,
Blood-splattered scenes I had seen the last 72 days!

Leanne Powley (13)
St Mary & St Joseph's School, Sidcup

The Swan

Looking over fields of roses like rubies as they glitter in the sun,
The birds nesting on the golden horizon,
Twittering happily,
The sun is a golden ring giving off light,
The swan glides gracefully over the smooth water,
Her opal-white babies gliding behind her,
A perfect end to a spring golden day.
The trees sway like a baby being cradled to sleep,
The silhouettes of foxes prowling over fields of golden roses,
Like ponies galloping gently.

Angela Gladding (13)
St Mary & St Joseph's School, Sidcup

Baby Girl

Baby girl you know my situation
My love for you could spread throughout the nation
If it was a shower it would cause major saturation.

God made you, God made me
That's why you and me were meant to be
We are as close as a nut and bolt
And in our relationship there hasn't been one fault.

I could spend my life with you
Without a day of being blue
I watch you when you sleep
And think of how much our love is and it is deep.

Joseph Chapman (12)
St Mary & St Joseph's School, Sidcup

Falling To The Earth

Falling down to the Earth,
Drip, drip, pitter-patter,
Trickling to the floor,
Running, running down a hill,
Flowing, moaning, sighing, groaning,
Gurgling and bubbling,
Merging in and out and round,
Bumping, thumping,
Eroding and sliding,
Over the precipice,
Over the edge,
Going down towards the Earth.
Flashing, crashing, bashing, dashing,
Down, down the cataract flows,
Writhing, diving, moving slyly,
Still it runs from peak to ground,
Leaping, flying, jumping, dying,
Tumbling, foaming, thundering,
Submerging, emerging,
Falling down to the Earth.

Naomi Russell (13)
The Grammar School For Girls, Wilmington

Time

Tick-tock, hands on a clock,
Time goes slow when you're watching the spot.
So keep on moving, finding things to do,
Life is too exciting to just stand still.
With every second we go forward,
Down the paths of our lives,
And then we take it for granted, until we rely on it to stop.
We do not value time, until we want it the most,
Has it been planned and is there order -
Are we part of someone else's scheme?
Answers we search for over time.
Wisdom comes with age, sometimes from making mistakes,
But will this give us the answers to all of our questions?
Whatever we do, time ticks on,
For all of us, time is not so long.

Sean Wright (11)
Tunbridge Wells Grammar School For Boys

Anger

Anger is something negative
Anger is something terrible
When you stare anger in the face, say *'Shoo!'*
Just be happy.

Anger is something stupid
Anger is something weird
When you get angry, think of something else,
Just be happy.

Anger is something strong
Anger is something that isn't nice
When someone gets angry, give them a chill pill,
Just be happy.

You shouldn't turn to anger.

William Ottway (12)
Tunbridge Wells Grammar School For Boys

What If?

I sometimes sit and wonder
What the world would be like
If everyone was black,
Or if everyone was white.
If everyone was a Hindu,
Or if everyone was a Sikh.
If everyone was English,
Or if everyone was Greek.
If everyone was happy,
Or if everyone was sad.
If everyone was good,
Or if everyone was bad.
If everyone was deaf,
Or if everyone was blind.
If everyone was evil,
Or if everyone was kind.
I sometimes sit and wonder
What the world would be like.

Howard Rickard (12)
Tunbridge Wells Grammar School For Boys

Motorbiking

M otorbiking, motorbiking,
O n the highway
T earing along the road
O nly myself to please.
R oaring around the bends,
B urning the tyres.
I feel the wind in my face
K eeping on the road.
I s it as much fun as you think?
N ipping through the traffic,
G etting everywhere on time!

Michael Wilkinson (11)
Tunbridge Wells Grammar School For Boys

My First Day At School

I wake with a start as the alarm bell rings,
Jumping out of bed I nearly land on the cat.
Turning on the light and blinking in the brightness,
When my eyes focus I see my brand-new blazer.
The thought comes into my head,
New school today!
Loads of changes await me.
No more blue shirts, just white,
Mustn't forget my dinner money,
Pack my things for the day.
Having to wear a tie,
Take my own writing things,
Blazer instead of sweater,
Walking out the door without my mum.
I chat to my friends on the way to the bus stop,
Hurrying them up not to miss the bus.
Arriving at the bus stop seeing all the new faces.
The bus arrives, there's a scramble for seats.
Suddenly I feel small again.
The journey is long but I'll have to get used to it.
We pull through the gates for the first time.
This is my new life now.

Nathan Durrant (11)
Tunbridge Wells Grammar School For Boys

Footie Mad

F ans rise and fall with every goal,
O ohs and aahs at every outrageous foul.
O pen spaces for the players to gallop into.
T urbulent conditions to play in throughout the winter.
B attling on as a team, whatever the score.
A mbitious players who all want to be victorious,
L ittle do they know the reaction of the millions watching,
L ovely football, the high of the winter.

Matthew Watts (12)
Tunbridge Wells Grammar School For Boys

Everlasting Seasons

Winter, what is winter?
Is it the snow-topped trees or
Maybe, the chilling breeze?
Kind greetings all the time,
The dew on the grass will always shine.
What is winter, may I ask?

Spring, what is spring?
Is it the flowers growing
Or the sweet smell flowing?
Baby lambs growing away,
Tales of Easter and that special day?
What is spring, may I ask?

Summer, what is summer?
Is it the blazing hot sun?
Kids outside all having fun.
Summer holidays, most people's rests,
All kinds of birds building nests?
What is summer, may I ask?

Autumn, what is autumn?
Will the leaves all fall and
Make the trees look small?
Birds flying to get away,
It's getting dark at the end of the day.
What is autumn, may I ask?

Paul Weatherall (11)
Tunbridge Wells Grammar School For Boys

Season's Feelings

As the flowers in spring start to blossom,
it makes me feel merry and joyful.
As I run in the woods listening to the birds singing,
they sound chirpy and cheerful.

As I play football on the grass,
with the sunrays all around me.
I feel the energy pumping through me
as I speed along the grass.

Autumn is a great time of year,
at least for me.
As the wind blows the conkers
from the trees.

As the snowflakes fall in wintertime,
it makes my body quiver.
As I wait at the bus stop,
it makes my bones shake and shiver.

Dean Weller (11)
Tunbridge Wells Grammar School For Boys

Autumn

The summer sun is fading
Beautiful summer flowers are falling,
Nights are getting colder with Jack Frost.
The cupboards are open
And the blankets are coming out.
Green leaves, dropping and dying,
Even though they still have magnificent colours.
In the morning, spiders are snoring,
Cobwebs appear overnight.
We know autumn's near,
We know autumn's here!

Peter Tubb (11)
Tunbridge Wells Grammar School For Boys

My Mate Rob

My mate Rob is really cool,
Every Sunday we go and play football.
He comes and collects me in his car,
It's just as well we don't need to go far!

He's 25, now that's a fact,
All his hair and teeth still seem intact.
We always have a laugh and mess about,
My mum says she'll give us both a clout!

We play the PlayStation and watch videos,
But all too quickly it's time to go.
We pack up our stuff and out the door,
Back in the car with Rob's foot to the floor.

We get back just in time for dinner,
My mum's Sunday roast is always a winner.
We end up flicking sweetcorn and stuff,
Often calling each other's bluff.

After dinner, I go off to bed
I feel so tired, I might be dead.
Rob stays up with my mum, till late,
But I don't mind, I think he's great!

Matthew Woodgate (11)
Tunbridge Wells Grammar School For Boys

Moving Things

The train goes past
I've never seen anything go so fast
As it goes past, I'm blown back
Straight into a gigantic sack

A plane goes overhead
I've never seen anything go so high
It's even higher than my shed
As it goes by, my ears go pop
I wish I was at home, buying sweets at the shop.

Daniel Wood (12)
Tunbridge Wells Grammar School For Boys

Teachers

Teachers, teachers, teachers,
Always having a moan.
They'll tell you off for anything
Even mumble or groan.

Untidy work, talking or plain laziness,
These are all crimes you can do for
The teacher to like you less.

I know what you're thinking and
You want to get your own back, but
All that is going to happen is
You're going on the detention rack.

Teachers, teachers, teachers,
There is nothing that you can do
From the teacher taking control
Of you!

Jamie Watson (12)
Tunbridge Wells Grammar School For Boys

What?

It was dark,
Creepy shadows moved.
I was only getting some fresh air,
Suddenly, a mystical light appeared,
Leaves rustled under heavy boots.
The eerie light disappeared.
The moth magnet faded,
Something tugged at my leg,
I looked down -
It looked up
Then it scuttled away!
The weird light appeared again
The only evidence was a soft, shiny material
Hanging from thorn bushes -
It was dark!

Alan Wanders (11)
Tunbridge Wells Grammar School For Boys

The Giant Eel

It lurks under the water,
Sleeps day and night,
Waits until some sailors come past,
Then gives them quite a fright.

The giant eel waits eleven years,
Then moves to another lake,
There it finds a place to sleep
And comes out when it awakes.

Its massive tail
And massive eyes,
Give the sailors
A huge surprise!

Suddenly a battle starts,
The giant eel versus people.
The eel dies
And leaves the village peaceful.

Sam Dowson (11)
Tunbridge Wells Grammar School For Boys

Roller Coaster

As I got on, it was very still
Gradually it started to fill
It moved at a very slow rate
Excitedly I chatted to my mate
I gradually climbed to the top of a hill
All the passengers sat very still.

It began to go as fast as it could
I nervously hung on to the wood
Then it flung around a corner
It was as hot as in a sauna
Everyone screamed, boy they were scared
I only went on because I was dared!

Gradually it stopped, relief was shared.

Jamie Gill (12)
Tunbridge Wells Grammar School For Boys

The Spy Rabbit

Beneath the surface of the Earth,
Far, far under, hidden,
A big, thick, fur coat sits,
The rabbit lies in deep sleep,
Waiting for sunlight to appear.

The morning comes and the moonlight goes,
The spy of the underground,
Comes out to play,
Jumping through fields,
Searching for food.

Digging up gardens,
Eating vegetables,
Cautiously munching,
Keeping company,
Out of his way.

Big, long, floppy ears,
Razor, outstretched claws,
Twitching his nose,
Snuggling in hay,
Resting his miniature legs.

Travelling once more,
Day after day,
Munching with his long teeth,
Digging deep underground,
To spy.

Protects himself against all evil,
In the deep, dark forests,
Then shudders, frozen
And stands there all night long.

Christopher Davies (11)
Tunbridge Wells Grammar School For Boys

Jealousy

God the Creator, gave us the gift of the Earth,
And put Adam and Eve on it, to give birth.
To us, their grandchildren
God's grandchildren,
But we always want to be like others.
Jealousy is a sin,
Is a no win.

He gave us the laser-blue sky,
The sparkling seas
The dazzling sun,
This wonderful world.
But we always want to have the same as others.
Jealousy is a sin,
It is a no win.

Mankind has made things
To love like crazy, like sport.
God gave us those ideas
God gave us all that joy -
But still we want to be better than others.
Jealousy is a sin,
It is a no win.

We always want more,
We always want to know the score.
We always put ourselves first,
That's what jealousy is -
It's a sin.
But Jesus gave us the greatest gift,
Better than them all.
Forgiveness.

Benjamin Watts (12)
Tunbridge Wells Grammar School For Boys

My First Race

I step into my lane,
There are butterflies in my stomach.
My heart is pounding,
The starter blows his whistle.

'On your marks!
Set!'
Bang!
The gun goes and we're off!
They're all ahead of me!

My arms are pumping,
My legs are working.
My breath is rasping,
My feet are thumping on the ground.

I come past one, then another
And two more, and another!
I'm in second place now, I'm catching the leader.
I pass him at the line!
Yes! The gold medal is mine.

Andrew Skiller (12)
Tunbridge Wells Grammar School For Boys

Bad Dog!

Dark and cold, moonlight on the ground,
Silence shattered by banshee-like sound.
Jaw through flesh, the ear-splitting scream,
Tranquillity shattered, like nightmare breaking through dream.
Unchecked blood spills from wound,
Pulse will go cold before too soon.
Woman lies dead, no one to help,
The predator skulks away, emitting nothing but a yelp!

Will Tompsett (12)
Tunbridge Wells Grammar School For Boys

Remembrance

R elentless fighting for no reason at all
E veryone wondering about the wicked waste of life
M en standing in boats, you can see the fear in their eyes
E verywhere the spectre of death hangs all around
M emories of home, a barrier to the war
B ang! Millions of lives taken with one single shell
E verywhere the loneliness envelops them all
R elentless, pointless, needless war!

T anks rolling across the ground, ready for action
H undreds of men lying there, dead!
E verywhere you look death hangs in the air.

L imping across the battlefield just missing the bullets
O rdinary men in the extraordinary horror of war
S tiffened bodies on the dark, bloody ground.
T heir loved ones don't know if they're dead or alive.

H eroic men, fighting for their lives
E ver hopeful that death will leave them alone
R eaching for life that is handed to a few
O ld men at home, remember their wars, whilst
E verywhere - poppies, the colour of blood.
S orrow and sadness. We must remember.

Nicholas Wallis (11)
Tunbridge Wells Grammar School For Boys

People In The World

Some people are not as lucky as we are,
Some people in the world have nothing,
Whilst we can have anything we want.
Shouldn't we give something to them?

While we have wars against the poor,
We look down on their fear.
We are the legs, they are the hips.
We are a family.

James Yardley (11)
Tunbridge Wells Grammar School For Boys

The Speedy Car Went Through The Streets

Going around the corners fast,
Flashing up the bright green grass,
A traffic light just turned red,
It flattens the people instead.
The cops are coming, what will it do?
It turns into a passing zoo!
It waits until the police have gone,
Then it zooms and carries on.
Then a Lotus suddenly appears,
The cars race, then disappear.
Then they enter another road,
The only victim was a toad.
The cops are coming again,
Then they both flatten a hen.
Now the police have had enough,
Things are going to get tough.
A police car rams into a car,
Knocking the other one very far.
'This is enough!' a policeman said.
'I'm going home and going to bed!'

George Fisk (11)
Tunbridge Wells Grammar School For Boys

My Poem Of Thoughts

In our English lesson we were told to write a poem.
I tried to write about an alleyway, but it didn't work,
My mum told me to write about my first day at school
But I couldn't remember much.
My older sister told me to write a sad poem
But I'm not good at writing emotional stuff,
My younger sister told me to write a nonsense poem
But I couldn't think of anything funny.
I asked my dad but he was busy,
I asked my dog but she just barked,
Here I sit writing my poem of thoughts.

James Dorricott (11)
Tunbridge Wells Grammar School For Boys

The World Of Autumn

The autumn haze of colour
Dancing leaves, brighten the sky
And the land is littered with fiery colours
The reds, oranges and crispy golden browns
Children run about, jumping into the eternal fields of colour
As cushions erupt around them
A mist of leaves jumps up
Dancing in the frosty autumn air
The wind pulls the trigger again
Another cushion explodes
More leaves are whipped up around them.

A heavenly beam of light appears
Creating a rainbow from the morning dew
And the landscape is a collage of leaves
The autumn artist is at work
The leaves sprout wings and they fly
Like birds they are soaring through the evening sky
The autumn artist starts to paint another part
Of his beautiful painting
The sun starts to set
The pink, orange blanket lays itself across the once, blue sky
And the autumn pictures fade into the darkness of the night.

Sam Tanner (12)
Tunbridge Wells Grammar School For Boys

Scaredy-Cat

I've just returned from school again,
it is another Friday.
Soon I'll get into my box
and again I'll hide away.

I guess you're wondering
why I hide?
If I come out, it's suicide!

My room's a death trap,
especially the floor,
with germs and bacteria
and much, much more.

Mum's room is just as bad,
it lingers in my head.
There's something living under there
that great big double bed.

The bathroom's not the best of places,
it's not where I choose to go.
There's a creature in the toilet,
my uncle told me so.

I hate to think of the other rooms,
you really don't need to know
anything about a place
you never should need to go.

If you asked my favourite room,
I'd whip you with my socks.
I'd shout at you extremely loud
and say that it's *my box!*

Alex Dove (12)
Tunbridge Wells Grammar School For Boys

Ode To A Toaster

Oh beautiful toaster
I do admire
The way you set my house on fire.
I love the way you singe my feet
And half the bushes on my street.
I adored the way you killed my mice
And burned my hands, not once but twice!
At this I can always boast
The way you always blacken my toast.
Oh fantastic toaster, I do hail,
The way you burned my dog's tail.
I cherish your flames blue and red
The ones that scorched my kitten's head.
I praise the way you sizzle my nose
And make it as red as a rose.
The first time we met, oh darling toaster
I felt I was on a roller coaster.
Oh toaster, won't you be my Valentine
And make my toast, just in time!

Jonathan Woolley (11)
Tunbridge Wells Grammar School For Boys

One Visit . . .

One visit to the zoo,
Makes you want to build a canoe
One visit to the park.
Makes you want to build Noah's Ark,
One visit to the car lot,
Makes you want to build a yacht.
One visit to the Diner
Makes you want to build a liner,
One visit to the foyer,
Makes you want to build a Destroyer,
All in all if you read this quick.
You may feel a bit seasick!

Robert Whittaker (11)
Tunbridge Wells Grammar School For Boys

The Moonlit Cove

The starlit beach, oh what a sight,
Beautiful in the sparkling light.
Frozen lakes trap the fish,
The curve of the lakes looks like a dish.
Oh wondrous cove covered in sand
Why are you there? What are you for?
Gaze into the diamond sky
The morning is nigh
The night comes to rest.
Day dawns and a new cove is seen,
The sunshine destroys the peace of the night.
All the tourists gather for fun.
The sun goes down and the night reigns supreme.
For now, until the morning where the cycle of light continues again.
Later that night a scene is viewed.
Could this be déjà vu?
The starlit beach, oh what a sight.
Beautiful in the sparkling light.

Michael Smith (13)
Tunbridge Wells Grammar School For Boys

It Would Be Good To Fly

It would be good to fly,
At least before I die.
It would be fun to soar
It will not be a bore.
Flying would be fun,
Right up to the sun.
I would not need a plane,
I would not need a train.
I'd really like to try,
It would be good to fly.

Philip Tremenheere (12)
Tunbridge Wells Grammar School For Boys

Getting To School

I got up in the morning, to the smell of burning toast,
To the sound of my dogs barking, at the fella from the post.
I strain my head to see, what the time is on my clock,
'Flippin' heck! I'll miss the bus, it's nearly seven o'clock.'
I scramble to my feet and tear into my clothes.
'Quick, quick! I've got to get ready, it's already time to go.'
I run downstairs to brush my teeth and slip into my shoes,
It's amazing how much damage happens, when you have
                                                      an over-snooze!
I hit the porch, sprint down the path, no time to cruise or glide.
Then suddenly, my fate is sealed, I've left my bag inside!
So I run back into the hall and pick up my heavy luggage,
This homework is as valuable as fifty golden nuggets.
Then I stagger towards the car and pass out on the floor,
I used up all my energy on slamming shut the door.
Eventually I got to school, fell asleep in every lesson.
I had to do a litter pick and after-school detention.

Michael Lever (12)
Tunbridge Wells Grammar School For Boys

Elvis

E lvis
L oved by everyone,
V alentine of girls all over,
I dol of fans everywhere from second to none.
S tates of America was where he began his life.

P eople round the world cried that fateful day
R ocked the world over until August 13th.
E ndless records bought by millions all over the globe
S ounded like the only person ever to save us with a song.
'L ittle Less Conversation' mixed by JXL but not original,
E nd of his career was in 1977 when he died of a drug overdose,
Y oung when he died, the whole world in misery, struck by darkness.

George Williams (11)
Tunbridge Wells Grammar School For Boys

The Start Of My Day

I wake up in the morning
At first I am still yawning
I sit up in my bed
And shake my sleepy head
I stand up on the floor
And wish I'd slept some more
I get into the shower
And stay there for half an hour
My mum begins to shout
My time is running out
I dry myself and dress
Leaving my room in a mess
I fill myself with toast
And go pick up the post
At a quarter to eight I walk
To meet my friends and talk
My school day starts once more
As I step through my form room door.

Kristian Wilson (11)
Tunbridge Wells Grammar School For Boys

My Goldfish Cole

A very wet pet is the goldfish
I thought as he swam around his bowl
One day he jumped out
And that was the end of Cole
Cole has been dead a very long time now
We buried him long ago
We buried him in the vegetable patch
He made the flowers grow
Now we have a very big cabbage
And peas as big as a toad
But now Cole is dead
The goodness in him will
Forever more grow.

George Cramer-Todd (11)
Tunbridge Wells Grammar School For Boys

The House

I always wondered what's in there -
The big, old, empty house?
So one day, in the dead of night,
I crept up the hill, like a mouse.

I always wondered what's in there -
The big, old, empty house?
I look up at the house and
I'm still wondering, what's in there?

So one night, I crept up to the house,
Like a mouse.
Without a fright, I crept up to the door,
Still wondering, what's in there?

As I opened the door, all I could see
Were very dusty floors,
Cobwebs all over the walls, the door
Slams behind me and I jump with fright.

I climb up the flight of stairs
With my hair on end.
Standing on the dark landing, shaking all over,
With one door at the end of the hall.

Walking towards the door
Now thinking, *what's in there?*
Drawing closer to the door,
Not knowing what to expect.
Then the door opens . . .

Shaun Drury (11)
Tunbridge Wells Grammar School For Boys

Fear

Filled with fear
Facing a shark,
It's thirty feet long
And the area is dark.

The shark has big teeth
It's ready to attack.
Fear has got to you
And you start to move back.

Then the shark is off,
It goes for you.
Fear is near
And jaws are ready to chew.

Your life flashes before you,
You think of the ones you love.
Then back to the real world
And there's only water above.

But the shark goes past you,
Your heartbeat stops.
You turn around
And your pulse rate drops.

The shark has got your leg,
You wrestle to get it back.
You see bloody water
And you feel a crack.

Here comes the end,
The shark is being fed.
You want to say goodbye to the world -
But you've lost all thoughts in your head.

Tim Riley (13)
Tunbridge Wells Grammar School For Boys

The Bandit Granny

She's a real old hag
Has a shotgun in her bag
She hobbles down the street
With jet packs on her feet.

She needs a cheap gift
So she decides to shoplift
She hobbles in a hardware shop
Gets a hello from the local cop.

She picks up the gift
Which she found hard to lift
She got out the gun
The boss began to run.

She took all the money
And thought it was very funny
She jet-packed round the store
Breaking the speed law.

She got all her bags
And grabbed a pack of fags
She then stole a car from the market
But the silly thing was, she couldn't park it.

She's a real old hag
Had a shotgun in her bag
She hobbles down the street
Now looking like a freak.

Dominic Tunstill (11)
Tunbridge Wells Grammar School For Boys

Darkness

The predator that follows wherever you go,
The presence never ends, through trouble and woe.
Nothing can stop it haunting the night,
Wherever, whenever, prepare for a fight.

A stalker of the day following closely,
The presence follows and feels quite ghostly.
Goes through holes, tunnels, under windows and doors,
Around hills and mountains, over bogs and moors.

The feeling of terror as you trudge down the road,
The figure behind you cannot be slowed.
You try to move faster, your energy is lost,
Nothing will work now, all hope is lost.

Your energy is gone, you're caught in his trap,
The footsteps get louder, you hear a loud *clap!*
The gun goes off, you breathe your last breath.
You look down at your feet and fall back to rest.

This shows what darkness can do to the mind,
It can deceive and trick you until you find that
You wake up at home, all snuggled in your bed,
But suddenly you feel that feeling of dread.

The predator is following wherever you go,
The presence never ends through trouble and woe.
Nothing can stop it haunting your night,
Get ready, you'd better be prepared for a fight!

Ed Brooks (12)
Tunbridge Wells Grammar School For Boys

That Girl

I watch her walk up her drive
Her legs move confidently
Her hair covers her pure white neck
She closes the door, shutting me out . . .

I see her in the corridor at school
I see her in the classroom
Her blue eyes light up the room
Her fingers move gracefully across the page
I see her cross the road
I see her disappear . . .

I see her parents weeping
I see her rose hairband
I saw her trying to cross the road
I knew I could not save this girl
I now see her in her silent grave.

William Bailey & Declan D'Arcy (12)
Tunbridge Wells Grammar School For Boys

My Sunset

My sunset is like a desert
With the wind swooping up all the sand
Making orange clouds across the sky

My sunset is like the sea
With the waves smashing against the rocks
Blue sky mixed with golden sand

My sunset is like a fire
With smoke coming up in black clouds
Among the roaring orange flames

Now the fire is out
Now the sea is calm
Now the sand is still
Out peeks the moon
With the stars by its side.

Andrew Wood (11)
Tunbridge Wells Grammar School For Boys

My Girl
(Dedicated to Charlotte Scott)

You're the light at the end of the darkest tunnel,
The brightest star in the sky.
You're a flower in blossom all year round
You're that mountain peak on high.

I love you more with each day that goes by,
I love everything you do
Why can't your parents just accept
I'm crazy about you.

You're my hope in times of worry and need,
An incentive to carry on.
Being with you is like being in Heaven,
But my heart aches when you're gone.

A life without you is no life at all,
I need you with me forever.
You're my little lady for as long as can be,
I will leave you never.
You don't know how much I love you.

Edward Hallford-Nye (13)
Tunbridge Wells Grammar School For Boys

Homelessness

Cold feet, no sleep
Bruised head, stone bed
No dosh, never wash
Wet, damp, stomach cramp
Freezing cold, I'm not bold
Shop doors, tiled floors
Listen out, for lager lout
Peed on, money gone
No loo, life's blue
Attacked again, by drunk men
Homelessness, what a mess.

Jake Bambrough (12)
Tunbridge Wells Grammar School For Boys

Death! A Poem To Wake The Dead

It's come for you,
Sliding and creeping,
Ever closer.
Waiting and hungry
It's wanting you
To die . . .

It's come for you,
Striding ever faster.
Closer to you,
You can't run.
It's excited and anxious,
Hungry for you
To die . . .

Death has come,
Groping madly for you.
Until it finds you
Wanting to pull you
Down into the pit of wretchedness
From where it came
To die . . .

Now it's got you
It can taste you,
Hungry for you,
Wanting you to
Succumb to the darkness
To die . . .

Locked in its jaws,
Now you're helpless.
Death's got you -
Like a rabbit in a
Fox's jaw!
Death's not one
To let go . . .

Now you're falling,
Drowning.
Death is dragging you
Through an ocean of blackness.
To where?
Who knows . . .
But the dead!

Max Richards
Tunbridge Wells Grammar School For Boys

Stealth

It was midnight.
Next door's black tomcat was out hunting.
I could see its stealthy silhouette,
Sneaking along the damp, soft grass.
You could tell it wasn't going to go home hungry,
By the way it jumped up onto the fence so elegantly
And without a sound.
Its large nocturnal eyes glinted in the moonlight
For any sudden movement,
Its ears ever listening.
It soared through the air as it jumped down to the ground.
With its tail twitching it sensed a movement up in the tall tree
In my garden.
As quick as a bullet it jumped onto the lawn
And started to climb the old oak,
Within a few seconds it reappeared at the bottom of the tree
With a sparrow in its mouth.
Then it sneaked into the shadows to feast upon its catch.

Calum Duncan (11)
Tunbridge Wells Grammar School For Boys

The Electric Shopping Cart

Bad boy racer Grandad
Tearing round the turns
Racing to the bakery
Pit stop on return.

Bad boy racer Grandad
Speeding down our street
Go-faster stripes on slippers
Tyres steaming with heat.

Bad boy racer Grandad
Sneaking through the lights
Sees a bright police car
And speeds on out of sight.

Bad boy racer Grandad
His battery almost flat
Takes another pit stop
And can't resist a nap.

Cameron Dall (12)
Tunbridge Wells Grammar School For Boys

Going To Jamaica

I'm going to Jamaica as fast as I can,
I'm going to Jamaica to get a tan.

I'm going to Jamaica to have some fun,
I'm going to Jamaica to find the sun.

I'm going to Jamaica, I'm going on a holiday,
I'm going to Jamaica I'm sure I'm going to stay.

I'm going to Jamaica to hire a yacht,
I'm going to Jamaica if you like it or not.

I'm going to Jamaica to see the sea,
I'm going to Jamaica, will you come with me?

Oliver Ward (11)
Tunbridge Wells Grammar School For Boys

The Seasons

The wind whistled through the trees,
Lifting away the frosty leaves.
The proud old trees stand stern and tall.
The wind blows away the grey, cold clouds.
Making a whisper.
No other sounds.

The sun starts to break,
It shines on the lake.
Warm or cold,
The trees are still old.
Hats and gloves
Get put away.
Children come out
And start to play.

The sun is strong
And the days are long,
The flowers grow and
The grass we mow.
We swim all day
The sun shines away.

Kids back to school
They try to act cool.
The horrid cold comes back,
Out comes the coal sacks.
The rain starts to fall,
On the old rustic wall.

But no need to fear -
They rotate every year.

Matthew Grainger (12)
Tunbridge Wells Grammar School For Boys

Autumn

Summer has ended, autumn has come,
Leaves start falling off trees and the wind blows them everywhere.
Conkers start to form and acorns drop from their trees,
Children finding conkers under leaves, while *crunch, crunch*
As they walk
It starts to get cold.
People leave parks,
Because of the darkness.
At night you could hear the wind and rain slashing on the window,
When you wake up, there is frost over the grass.
Remember it's 'hats, gloves and scarves' time now and
When October has nearly finished, Halowe'en starts to rise,
People buy costumes.
Then *bang! Bang! Bang!* November the fifth has arrived.
Fireworks start in the sky -
Red, blue and yellow - all different colours.
Not long now and winter will be here.

Tom Watson (11)
Tunbridge Wells Grammar School For Boys

Wild And Lone

Those sharp, black claws,
The brown fur, the grey tail.
The wolf lives without a cause,
Trying to find us, to tell his tale.

Those sharp, yellowing teeth,
The silver back, the glaring eyes.
The wolf lives alone, in peace,
Trying to find us, to tell his tale.

Those powerful, massive limbs,
The bristling fur, the domination.
The wolf pads along, searching, searching,
Trying to find us, to tell his tale.

Michael Ells (13)
Tunbridge Wells Grammar School For Boys

Everlasting Torture

The trees lie blackened, scarred by death.
The grass is dissolved, poisoned by disease.
The birds never sing, killed by the fires of Hell,
Paradise is lost, never to return.

The epidemic spreads from inch to inch,
Field to field, town to town.
Creeping, swallowing, engulfing everything in its path.
Animals, fish and birds perish, swamped in the blackness.

Human lives are taken; one by one,
Snatched from the undergrowth.
Taken! Going, going, going, gone!
Lost forever in the wilderness, struggling to revive.

Lingering in every place and remaining in disguise,
The pollution sweeps through the land, waiting for a prize.
You are the target for the next massacre,
Ready to be carted away to Hell, captured in everlasting torture.

For this mess that is created
Was an apparent result of us.
The human power and group, has destroyed the world forever,
And it is us who will suffer the consequences
That are likely to result in death.

Jack Stookes (12)
Tunbridge Wells Grammar School For Boys

The Race

We're all on the line,
Waiting for the gun,
It goes off with a *bang!*
The race has begun.

I get a decent start,
I'm in third place,
I speed up a bit,
I'm winning the race.

We're halfway through,
But the others are catching up,
I have to hold this lead,
Or I won't win the cup.

The finish line's getting closer,
I put on a burst,
I'm a metre away,
I'm going to come first.

I cross the line,
With tears on my face,
Now I know what it's like,
To win a race.

Tom Parrish (12)
Tunbridge Wells Grammar School For Boys

Moving

We move here and we move there,
We move just about everywhere.
But when we get there,
It's as if the cupboard was bare
And you don't know what to do.
So you move on to the next one,
As if nothing had ever happened.
Animals have the hardest lives.

Ted Sardar (13)
Tunbridge Wells Grammar School For Boys

Bees

Bees, the wonderful things,
Making honey all day,
They slave away,
In the hive,
Making honey all day.

The workers forage,
For nectar and pollen,
To store in the hive today,
They work till night,
Then they rest,
Having made honey all day.

They work so hard,
For us to sell,
Big jars full of honey
And all we think they do is sting.

Roger King (12)
Tunbridge Wells Grammar School For Boys

School

School crowded
Everywhere
Every place
Every stair
People squashed
Upon the door
Against the wall
Or on the floor
People pull
Shirts tear
Trousers rip
We don't care
School crowded
Everywhere
Every place
Every stair.

Joshua Brice (12)
Tunbridge Wells Grammar School For Boys

Love

Love is all around us,
Love is everywhere,
Even if we can't see it,
It's waiting there.

It pulls people close,
Too close to see,
So if you resist the love given,
You'll feel so small like a pea.

Love is innocent,
Love is caring,
Love means that you're going to have to,
Be quite daring.

Love is like the wind,
You can't see it - but you can always feel it,
Blowing round your heart,
Right from the start.

Love, though, can be bad,
Bad enough to kill,
You really can't fight it,
But you know you will.

Love causes war,
Love causes hate,
So if you fight the love,
It will bring you to your fate.

Phil Selwood (13)
Tunbridge Wells Grammar School For Boys

It's Football!

Football is my favourite sport,
It beats all the others by miles,
So here is a poem for you,
It's football!

You're kicking a ball,
Maybe against a wall,
Tackling your man,
Like in the plan.
Run really fast,
So you can get past,
The player advancing on you.

You're calling a name,
To help win that game,
To put your team on top.
You have to shoot,
With either boot,
To score a wonderful goal.

You cross that ball,
Towards someone tall,
To head it into the net.
It's football!
A yellow or a red card,
Might give you an early bath,
But still cheer your team on,
Don't walk 'til you're gone.
It's football!
It's football!
It's football!

Michael Hodges (12)
Tunbridge Wells Grammar School For Boys

The Thing

A boy is sleeping on the floor,
He hears a noise from the front door.
So tiptoes down to see what it is
And he thinks it's only his dog (called Fizz).

Ssh! Don't wake the parents up,
He's thirsty, so he gets a can of 7 Up.
There it goes again, but he wouldn't dare,
To go and see what's over there.

Never mind, let's go back to bed,
'I wonder what it is?' he said,
It sounded like a ghost. G-g-ghost!
Look, there's a shadow by the lamp post.

He sneaks out again to take a glance,
The thing looks like it's doing a dance!
He sees a pair of big green eyes
And hair (it's eating two apple pies).

He steps into the light, he can't believe
It's his long-lost uncle Steve!
He hasn't seen him for ten whole years,
He starts to cry and wipes away his tears.

Andrew Brown (13)
Tunbridge Wells Grammar School For Boys

The Bad Guy

Invading countries in his path,
The Nazi dictator wanted some land.
He was given an ultimatum by Churchill
But continued with what he had planned.

This, of course, triggered war,
And loads of guns were aimed.
Thousands of souls were wiped away
And Hitler was the one to be blamed.

Thomas Wood (12)
Tunbridge Wells Grammar School For Boys

Some Things

Some things in life are very dear to me . . .
Such things as flowers coated by the rain,
Or patterns traced by waves upon the sea,
Or crocuses peeping through snow again.

The holy iridescence of a gem,
The moon's cool shining opalescent light,
Azaleas and the sweet smell of them
And the scent of honeysuckle at night.

And many sounds are also dear . . .
Like wind that sings among the orchard trees,
Or seagulls calling from above the pier,
Or crickets singing high-pitched melodies.

But far more important than all surmise,
Are sudden teardrops in your eyes.

Daniel Francis (12)
Tunbridge Wells Grammar School For Boys

The Weasel

Why do I raid dustbins?
Why am I forced to steal?
The answer to the questions is
I am a *weasel!*
I stalk the streets at night
Raiding bins and having a fight
But sometimes I look for a better meal
Other than fish bones, I want something real!
So I sneak into restaurants pinching chickens and jelly
And when I'm kicked out again I run away with a full belly.
All I am is a robber, stealing day and night
I stole some eggs yesterday and gave the chicks a fright.
I run off into the twilight feeling pleased, but night has gone
I scamper down my burrow and sleep the whole day long.

Tim Drake Brockman (11)
Tunbridge Wells Grammar School For Boys

Dancing Lover

Moving gracefully with every step,
The constant rhythm in our feet,
We moved so smoothly as the teacher kept
Our heart's desire to keep the beat.

As time moved on the pace quickened,
We danced faster, the music in mind.
She clenched my hand as she slipped and . . .
The beat we lost and couldn't find.

We slowed our speed, the mistake in the past,
Flowing, floating our feet off the ground.
Never in my life has my heart beat so fast,
The blood in our heads drowned out the sound.

The bell was ringing, the class like no other
Was over and gone, just like another.
And as I walked away from the smother
I knew I could never find another dancing lover.

James Perrett (13)
Tunbridge Wells Grammar School For Boys

Another Bad Day

A schoolboy goes to school, alone, alone,
He had missed the bus, a groan, a groan,
Forty minutes late, detention at lunch,
Bullied by some schoolboys, who gave him a punch.
Results of a test, bad marks in French,
PE, bad foul, red card, on the bench,
He catches a bus home, not a good thought,
A bundle had started and he got caught.
His bus pass ripped, he walked not far home,
He opened the door, as cold as a bone.
His dad was out of money, his mum ran away,
No free time, no fun, just another bad day.

Daniel Edgson Wright (12)
Tunbridge Wells Grammar School For Boys

A Poem About Writing A Poem

I've got to write a poem
but I don't know where to start.
The beginning seems a likely place
but I'm finding it quite hard.

I could write about the weather
or perhaps the raging sea.
What about my school friends -
maybe even me.

I could say what makes me happy
or things that make me sad.
About all the things that make me laugh
and those that make me sad.

What about the seasons
or sunny months like May.
I could just keep on writing
until I run out of things to say.

Sam Gregson-Williams (12)
Tunbridge Wells Grammar School For Boys

I Believe

I believe life is too short, time is ticking away
I believe you have to work hard to succeed
I believe that sweets taste so good because they are bad for you
I believe family is worth more than money or gold
I believe there will always be light during the day
I believe in freedom for everyone, no matter who they are
I believe in giving and receiving in return
I believe that making people smile is the most important thing
I believe that being excluded is a feeling I do not wish to feel
I believe friends should be friends forever
I believe all ideas should be shared
I believe life is for living and enjoying.

Mark Eastwood (11)
Tunbridge Wells Grammar School For Boys

The Diker

Underneath thy endless deeps,
Undisturbed by the creatures above,
The diker lies in a dreamless sleep,
Quiet and thoughtful in his cave.
For to guard the treasure he once found,
Invading his territory,
He awoke and swam up to the light he saw.
Up he went silent as a mouse,
A dignified tiger ready to pounce.
He approached some land
And lifted his flippers upon the sand.
He crawled through the jungle,
Through darkness and in light,
A huge, fierce boxer looking for a fight,
An anger swelled inside him,
A volcano about to erupt,
But still the diker came,
Through streams and over grass,
Until he came into a pass,
A mountain or a swamp?
But the diker carried on
Over pebble, over rock
Until deep in Scotland
He came to a loch.
He crawled into the water
And swam to the bottom
Where he rested again
A silent bird asleep,
Never again to come out of the deep.

Alex d'Albertanson (12)
Tunbridge Wells Grammar School For Boys

Subtle Murder

The click of the magazine,
The crack of it being cocked,
The careful aim of the untamed beast,
The black leather glove,
With the index finger,
Resting on the trigger,
Then the almighty roar
And an ear-splitting bang,
The glint of a small blurred gold object,
Flying through the air,
Perfectly aerodynamic,
The wind rushing,
Then the sad, dull thud
And the river of red liquid
Streams out like lava
And the body falls down,
Dead!

Will Moore (12)
Tunbridge Wells Grammar School For Boys

The Great White Shark

The great white shark is lurking in the deep,
He is searching for his prey.
He fancies a juicy seal, or maybe two.
He sees a shadow floating on the surface
And decides it will be his victim.
He rockets upwards towards the prey,
He has never missed before.
But this time his prey is too quick for him,
It speeds towards the shore.
He immediately takes pursuit,
But his prey gets there first.
The shark turns around
And surrenders to the depths of the ocean.

Stephen Dale (11)
Tunbridge Wells Grammar School For Boys

Motion

Motion, motion
Here I come
Motion, motion
Now I'm gone.

In the wind, I hear the voices
Travelling on the windswept air
The voices travelling without a care
The original form of motion.

The creaking of the axle
The crumbling of the stones
The cantering of the horses
The second form of motion.

The roaring of the engine
The spinning of the wheels
The pushing of the pedal
The ultimate form of motion.

The cocking of the gun
The pulling of the trigger
The flight of the bullet
The final form of motion.

Motion, motion
Here I come
Motion, motion
Now I'm gone.

Gordon Rieck (14)
Tunbridge Wells Grammar School For Boys

Teens

Teens,
Some are tall,
Some are small,
Teens,
I don't understand them.

Teens,
Some are grumpy,
Some are happy,
Teens,
I don't understand them.

Teens,
Fashion is all the rage,
They say it's about your age,
Teens,
I don't understand them.

Teens,
They are older then me,
They think I'm a pygmy,
Teens,
I don't understand them.

Teens,
Now I'm a teen,
I understand what they mean,
Teens,
I know what the mean.

Alex Day (11)
Tunbridge Wells Grammar School For Boys

Animals

Kangaroos are leaping,
Elephants are sleeping,
Rabbits are hopping,
Humans are jogging.

Spiders are crawling,
Snakes are hissing,
Monkeys are swinging,
Birds are singing.

Fish are swimming,
Bats are flying,
Cheetahs are speeding,
Moles are burrowing.

Bulls are charging,
Bees are buzzing,
Lions are roaring,
Tigers are pouncing.

Ryan Welby (11)
Tunbridge Wells Grammar School For Boys

Wimbledon

W ishing to play there,
 I mpossible to play there.
M ust see it,
B ut can't see it.
L ove to be there,
E ven though I can't be there.
D reaming to win,
O nly, I can't win it,
N o chance at all, or is there . . .

John Bone (12)
Tunbridge Wells Grammar School For Boys

Gangsters

As they run around town
Destroying whatever gets in their way
I stand there thinking, *why*?
Why do they destroy?
Whatever they destroy without dismay
They never think about where it's from
They just destroy.
They dance around with chunks of wood
And destroy like anyone could.
They wouldn't care if cheap or expensive
They would just destroy without dismay.
Statues would fall and crumble
Windows shattered into pieces
But shelters smashed and demolished
Cars wrecked and ruined
Libraries burnt down
Shops getting looted.
I don't understand why they do this
Or what their motive is.
All I know is they can't destroy me.

Declan Ellis (11)
Tunbridge Wells Grammar School For Boys

Flowing River

River flowing everywhere,
Running fast, it doesn't care.
Splish and splash, off the rocks,
It's coming down into the Docks.

Rushing down into the sea,
Buzzing round, just like a bee.
Journey's end is nearly here,
Travelling through a weir.

Thomas Williams (11)
Tunbridge Wells Grammar School For Boys

Growing Up

When I was a boy I was very small,
I looked upwards, craning my neck to look at you all.
I did not walk, but I could crawl, when I was very small.
I learned to talk at the age of one, my first word was 'daddydoodoo'.
My life moved on, but not that much,
My vocab changed to 'Mummy' and 'Daddy'.
When I was three I started playschool
And my co-ordination turned out to be great!
I loved to play on the climbing frame,
I loved the slide and loved to draw
And played different games much more.
When I was aged five I started my new school,
My teacher was called Mrs Brown, she'd tell us to sit down
And then read us a story.
In that year I learned to write, I also learned to read.
Story times on Fridays, we could bring a favourite toy
But when I brought Mr Snake I would tell a really long story.
My, fat, cat, dog, Bill, Mum and *Dad* were the words that I could write,
I'd write my words and read them out
And if I finished I would get a Smartie and a gold star.
When I moved up to junior school
I could do maths and history quite well.
My mum was very proud, my life was getting bigger
And I was learning more.
Now I'm aged eleven, my life is getting scary.
I'm working hard and enjoying it, now I don't only look up,
I look down at some as well.

Jamie Craig (11)
Tunbridge Wells Grammar School For Boys

Year 6 Boys' Relay

Our teacher held up the number forty-nine,
It was my race, the Year 6 boys' relay,
We all knew that we had a nifty team,
But that didn't stop the nerves.

We all got ready into our starting positions,
Everyone waiting for the whistle to go,
Our hearts were pounding,
Our bodies were shaking.

The whistle blew,
Our first runner was shooting down the track like a bullet,
All I had to do was wait for the next boy to hand the baton to me.

I watched the second runner charge towards me,
His face as red as an apple,
Blood rushing round his body
He was in the last ten metres,
I got ready to run.

He handed me the baton and I went flying off,
Adrenaline pumping through my body,
I let my legs carry me away
And before I knew it I was at the end,
I let go of the baton as I felt it hit the next runner's hand
Then watched him storm off.

I turned around puffing and panting,
I watched our fourth runner sprint down the track,
He was quite far ahead speeding to win,
He crossed the finish line and we had won, *we had won.*

Henry Everett (11)
Tunbridge Wells Grammar School For Boys

The Fiendish Dragon

The fiendish dragon dwells
in his cave far below ground.
His skin is harsh and bloated
like a toad
and his eyes are deep sockets,
hollow and sightless.

His claws are of steel
and his back is riddled
with all sorts of spines and blades.
His tail is long and bony,
long stripped of muscle.

His face is long, like an alligator
but his skin clings weakly to his bones
like pebbles and stones
in an old leather bag.

Deep inside him is a glow,
that stopped him turning to dust aeons ago.
As he wanders the endless labyrinths
that spark of evil begins to grow.

He crushes skulls and bones underfoot
as the floor is littered with dead vermin.
He tries to spread his bat-like wings
but the passageway is too narrow
and he lies back, defeated.

Richard Fallon (12)
Tunbridge Wells Grammar School For Boys

Football

The ball was placed on the centre spot
Players waiting for the whistle to blow
Hearts pounding
Faces red
With excitement raring to go.
The sound everyone was waiting for suddenly went off
Their players charged at top speed
Looking like bulls with horns
Their team was strong
But we fought back with all our might
Hoping their defence would fall
There was one player on their team
So strong and big he was
Then you look at me so small and weak
He could squish me in one step
And that's exactly what he did
He got the ball turned around
And pushed me out the way
I was so scared of that boy
That I asked my coach
If I could be subbed for a better player
This made all the difference
The new player scored three
And won us the game
I felt a failure to my team
They encouraged me from then on
And now I am the most improved
Player of the year.

Michael Dobereiner (11)
Tunbridge Wells Grammar School For Boys

Being Small

Being small is very hard,
With people looking down at you,
But when you get the gist of it,
You really can't start to quit.

Everything looks so big,
But it has a secret jig,
You storm through big and small,
Things to push and things to pull.

From tables and chairs,
To gorillas and bears
Your mind starts to go blank,
It is like walking off a plank.

So now you know how it is to be small,
Just like me,
If when you're older you turn out to be tall,
Just think that you are lucky.

So by now you should know how it is,
To be a very small kid,
So when you have got a spare minute,
Think what it's like to be me.

Ben Dahmen (11)
Tunbridge Wells Grammar School For Boys

My Autumn Poem

I woke up in the morning
with the scent of fresh air
and the sound of crispy rustling leaves.
I looked out of the window
and saw the bare branches and
my cold breath fog up the window.

I walked through the woodland
listening to the robins singing
and the sound of conkers
falling from trees.
I sat by the frosted lake
feeling fresh and gazing up
at the amber crispy leaves.
I got up and walked home
singing hymns and spinning sycamores.

When I got home I felt warmth
strike my face and the sound of fire
I walked in the living room and heard
the crackling of fire and I sat in front of
the fire and fell asleep.

Alan Haugh (12)
Tunbridge Wells Grammar School For Boys

My Feelings And Thoughts

Peaceful as snow,
Loud as thunder,
My thoughts lurk in the darkness of my mind,
Swift as the wind,
Slow as a snail,
My questions circle round my head.
When I'm angry I'm in a boiler,
My feelings are always hot or cold
But I can always see a light,
When I run I hit one thousand,
When I crawl I miss one,
However fast or slow I go
I shall always be happy,
When I weep I am so happy,
When I'm happy I weep so much,
When I play I laugh with joy,
When I sulk I'm cross with sorrow.
I always say I am what I am,
But I want to be someone else.

I have never understood myself and never shall.

Aaron Fariba (12)
Tunbridge Wells Grammar School For Boys

The War

Boom! 'Argh!'
Screams of pain are everywhere
As I hide behind the army tank,
Crouching like a jaguar, about to pounce on its prey,
I wonder, why is this happening?
Why should people die?

It is only land,
What is the point of dying for land?
All you can do is build, build, build
And pollute the world around us.

So I stood up
And took my horn.
Courageously I ran, straight to battle.
Twice I blew my horn and attention was all on me.
As guns pointed at my head, I feared I would soon be dead.

Without thinking I flung up my hands and said,
'Stop! Don't keep killing each other,
Just be friendly and share the land.'
Nobody listened.
In a flash of green and red,
I fell to the ground, finally dead.

Christopher Farrell (11)
Tunbridge Wells Grammar School For Boys

Homework

I've got to write a poem,
My teacher told me so.
It can be about anything
And I thought, *oh no, no!*

I'm absolutely hopeless,
I cannot write a thing.
This really is so difficult,
I'll give my friend a ring.

The words all seem to jump around,
My mind goes very blank.
I seem to try and make things rhyme,
Like sausages and plank.

I'll have to tell my teacher
It really is too bad,
I hope she doesn't tell me off,
I hope she isn't mad.

I've just read through my homework,
I can't believe my eyes,
Perhaps I'll make a poet some day -
Surprise, surprise, surprise!

Frank Anthony Ward (11)
Tunbridge Wells Grammar School For Boys

The End Of The Universe

The last of the dying suns blazed madly at death's door.
Black holes swallowed up the planets, a terrible black sore.
Planets battled for survival, but to no avail.
The world was becoming an empty black sail.

Two huge suns collided with disastrous force,
So ten planets changed their terrible course.
Like a gaping pocket,
Death swallowed an unfortunate rocket.

Then, the last three planets:
A moon - glistening like granite,
A sun - a burning ball of fire
And a blue-green planet sent to die.
With a glitter and a twirl,
All three dissolved into the infinite black.

Henry Dolling (11)
Tunbridge Wells Grammar School For Boys

My England

England's treasure chest of pleasure,
Country lanes, weather vanes,
Church spires, chamber choirs,
Tolling bells, old stone wells,
Fresh cream teas, gentle breeze,
Bramleys, Coxes, strawberry boxes.

England's growing, darkness showing,
Crowded train, incessant rain,
Postal strike, stolen bike,
Battered wife, mugger's knife,
Child abuser, heroine user,
Yardie shooting, riots, looting.

Will England's green and pleasant land
Survive despite the English man?

Hazel Levett (14)
Walthamstow Hall

Spot A Change?

London,
Once a city,
Now a ruined jungle of disused buildings and overcrowded streets,
No skyline left,
Just a mass of offices entwined into one,
Grease-lined packets spew onto the streets,
Rain water washing them into the heart of the jungle.

London,
Once a place to visit,
Now a bubble of polluted air,
Sucked into anyone who dares breathe,
Buildings marked with fumes,
Windows smashed with dirt,
Stairs crumble,
Locks rust and fall.

London,
Once a place of beauty and colour,
Now a mass of dirt and dust,
Streets layered in chewing gum,
Hotel signs hanging off their hinges,
Cigarette butts line the pavement,
Drunkenness fills the air.

London,
Once a place of life,
Now just an empty place,
People blank, minds only for money,
Houses abandoned,
Laughter not to be heard.

London.
What now?

Lauren Watson (14)
Walthamstow Hall

I Am A Forest

I am a forest, ancient and old
Where druids once came to worship and behold.

I am a forest, dark and dense
Many roots beneath me twisted and tense.

I am a forest with many shadows so deep
The flowers below me whisper and weep.

I am a forest reaching for the sun
Where life has ended and just begun.

I am a forest where the oak is king
Where from the shadows, the owls take their wing.

I am a forest full of nature's sound
The fearful cry of prey echoes around.

I am a forest where gloom shines through
In every nook and cranny, but with nothing to do.

I am a forest with many secrets to be told
The breeze sweeps through, light yet cold.

I am the forest where the fox lays underground
Where man walks through, moss muffling his sound.

I am a forest that is scared of man
Yet this is where he first began.

Gemma Cottis (12)
Walthamstow Hall

My Old House

I can see my old house from across my old street
As the leaves go crunch beneath my feet.

I raise my head to see the movement of a tree,
Its branches wave back as if remembering me.

If I close my eyes I can still find my way,
This was my street where I used to play.

Where the snow stung my face until the happiness I felt
Turned into tears as our fun began to melt.

And the sunny days meant running in the grass,
My friends far ahead, were they always so fast?

We stood in the cool breeze that rustled our hair,
Our lives were simple, never a care.

The blossom on this tree made us curious to know
Why the same tree looked so different not that long ago?

I look out at my old street and see leaves in a pile,
How I would have loved to jump in them and play again for a while.

Stephanie Pickerill (14)
Walthamstow Hall

Autumn

Its leaves rich, strong and vibrant, like a furnace glowing bright,
Gently drifting in the bleakness of the misty morning light,
Spiders' webs softly woven, silky strands, through the branches,
With the birds cooing sweetly in the trees.

Sapped trees strip off their fiery clothes, randomly to the ground,
Nests no longer hidden, camouflage removed, there for all to see,
                                        the source of summer sound.
Squirrels gather nuts on a carpet red and gold.
The morning dew still resting on the lawn.

Tanwen Evans (11)
Walthamstow Hall

Britain's Two Faces

As I sit on my swing,
I hear the silent banging of the woodpecker,
The lovely melody of the robin.
The evergreen grass swiftly dancing in
Beat with the wind.
In the distance a golden cornfield,
Its colour resembling a ring on a bride's delicate finger.
The tingle tangle of silk spiderwebs,
Carefully decorated with crystal dew.
Gently the rain trickles down and melts
God's beautiful drawing.

I am in the hustle and bustle of the streets.
Lights are flashing all around me.
I hear the gaggling of English people
Buzzing in my ear.
Figures blur past me, I get muddled and confused.
And all I want to do is sit on my swing in
Britain's first of his two faces.

Jessica Wrigley (11)
Walthamstow Hall

Southwold

Across the dunes, the town appears before me.
Perfect in its tidiness, its streets and its houses scrubbed with pride.
The lighthouse, solid and comforting, rises up between them,
                                                                                  protecting.

Beach huts glowing with individuality, line the promenade
And show an array of rainbow colours,
Each with names full of character and charm.

The fresh easterly wind blows across the beach,
The grey-green broth froths over the shingle and tumbles back
                                                                        down to the shore.

Up the estuary, the harbour with its jetties, like bones stuck
                                                         in the belly of a low tide mud.

Rosalind Mayes (13)
Walthamstow Hall

London To Brighton

The sun blazes on this isolated island,
The rays burning onto the buskers' still heads,
A penny flies through the air,
A child peering excitedly,
The silver statue begins to wave mechanically,
Cafés spill onto the cobbled streets of Covent Garden.

In the distance trains rumble,
My pace picks up.
On the train
Places rush past me,
London standing as I leave.
Large, ivy-covered houses pass by,
Yet the gardens still linger.

Soon I see the milky sea
Waving towards us.
The blackened sorrowful West Pier alone,
Whilst the colourful packed Palace Pier
Weighed down with rides
And children checking their height
Stand beside gleefully.

Gillian McCusker (15)
Walthamstow Hall

Held By The Lammerlaws

Hiding in the Lammerlaws,
Dashing through the thistle-bound grass and dancing
                                        dandelion clocks,
Into the rock cave supporting the mountainside,
The secluded place; different from any other.
Smaller, yet somehow more alive.

Sheltered in the Lammerlaws,
With a fire on the floor as the snow floats to the ground,
Alone with the world,
Distant; protected by this silver sheet.
Just beyond harm's grasp.

Undiscovered in the Lammerlaws,
Listening to the sea chant its monotonous song,
As it breathes in and then out,
Like clockwork; never ceasing.
Never at rest.

Far from the Lammerlaws,
Setting along the frost-bound track,
As the gloaming sets in,
As the shadows appear; all safety now gone.
Leaving the Lammerlaws alone by the sea.

Rosie Buist (12)
Walthamstow Hall

Another Tiger Is Lost

A mass of stripes slips through plants and trees.
Someone, somewhere holds their breath
As he passes them close by.
This skilful hunter is not deceived.

He hears their silent prayers,
Thoughts muttered under their breath,
The nervous pound of their heartbeats
Crash and echo in his ears,
The beads of sweat on their foreheads
Drench his fur like jungle rain,
Their human scent invades his nostrils,
Their presence, a spear, piercing his side.

His thick fur strikes up on end,
His feet carefully tiptoe towards them.
Then a clicking noise begins,
A smoky metal smell fills the air.
He stops.
Silent.
Still.
His senses tell him to run,
To flee deep into the undergrowth.
He hesitates,
Unsure whether to attack or take flight.

And then it's too late . . .
And there's nothing he can do,
But lie there,
And watch,
As the cruel, iron bars,

Encage him.

Abbie Kemsley (14)
Walthamstow Hall

Getting To Work

Holding your briefcase
clutching your phone
getting to work, you're not alone
catching the train to Charing Cross
shoulder to shoulder with the boss
no room to breathe
the train is packed
can't be late, you might get sacked
the hustle and bustle of busy commuters
you arrive at work
turn on computers
same routine, same old game
go to work, leave again
like robots we live, all year round
no time to stop, to look around.

Lucy Low (13)
Walthamstow Hall

A Closer Look

Green stems rise up and bloom into emerald umbrellas
Casting patterns on the murky water below.
Ivory lily flowers blossom above the water surface
Seemingly floating of their own accord.
Pondweed spirals its way slowly upwards
In a vain attempt to reach the light above.
Water cascades down from a nearby fall
Sending ripples into the surrounding shallows.

But when I stood up, all I saw was the muddy pond
At the end of our garden.

Miranda Kitchener (12)
Walthamstow Hall

Britain

I lay there still, on the ground,
Watching the clouds drift onwards over my head
Like a never-ending sea of grey.
I feel droplets of rain on my face.
A calm wind dances with the trees.
As the sun disappears below the horizon
The darker sky rakes over
And the moon smiles sweetly at me,
With its followers glimmering all around.
As the sky falls asleep, so do I.
The wind brushes my face like an icy hand
And the clouds conceal the starlight.
As the morning light creeps back again,
And the fresh smell of dew enchants me,
I proudly smile to myself,
Because no matter how dismal it can get
It will always be my perfect land.

Rachel Bullen (12)
Walthamstow Hall

Night

Night is like a lady sweeping over the Earth.
Comes dressed in black and covers everything,
Even the smallest cracks or the brightest suns.
And when she comes, people can no more see,
For their eyes are covered by her darkness,
Which sweeps over them like the ocean.
And like the ocean it seems to never end,
For the lady's robes are infinite,
Always veiling the Earth.
When the break of dawn approaches,
Her gowns only turn lighter.
For she is always walking on the Earth,
Clear, yet so invisible to us all.
And like the night, she is a mystery.

Gabi Groves (13)
Walthamstow Hall

Exmoor

The rolling hills of Exmoor
Stand up tall and rise above us,
Fixed since the dawn of time,
Only they can confirm the existence
Of the beast that wanders in the night.
Their secrets closely guarded,
Wind whips through your hair,
Ponies run free up there
Without a cause for concern,
The space is vast laid out in front of them,
No boundaries on their soles,
The smell so fresh, so sweet, so pure,
Colours are vibrant and bright,
Sun blazes down burning the dusty track,
Little red stone villages, idyllic basking in the sun
Burst with activity the morning of the hunt,
The red deer unaware of the events that may later come,
The valley of the bubbling spring
Rolling farmland and open moor,
That make up the beautiful sights of Exmoor.

Francesca Warrington (14)
Walthamstow Hall